THE MAYOR OF UPPER UPSALQUITCH

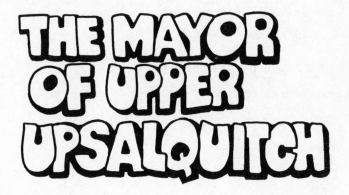

THE MAYOR OF UPPER UPSALQUITCH

John S. Crosbie

McGRAW-HILL RYERSON LIMITED

TORONTO MONTREAL NEW YORK LONDON SYDNEY JOHANNESBURG
MEXICO PANAMA DÜSSELDORF SINGAPORE SAO PAULO
KUALA LUMPUR NEW DELHI

THE MAYOR OF UPPER UPSALQUITCH

ISBN 0-07-077629-6

1 2 3 4 5 6 7 8 9 10   D73   10 9 8 7 6 5 4 3

Printed and bound in Canada

THIS BOOK IS DEDICATED

TO

THE STAR OF MY LIFE,

PATTY

AND THE SUPPORTING CAST:

KATIE, PETER, STEPHEN AND ANDREW.

SORRY, SILVER AND ZAK;
NO DOGS ALLOWED.

Wednesday January 1

A nice fresh diary and the first page crying for a resolution! So, unfortunately, are the various things still rumbling around inside my well-padded body. I was young once—until about ten after midnight last night. From then until the last guest left I grew older so rapidly that long before dawn I had passed by my true age. Awoke this morning to be greeted in the bathroom mirror by someone who looked like Grandpa Heber the day he discovered Grandma cutting up with the butcher.

New Year's Resolutions

1) I will never drink another drop, even if it's free.
2) I will stop taking advantage of people, even if they deserve it.
3) I will be a better, more generous man and an honest mayor.
4) I will never again look in a mirror on New Year's Day.

Quite a party. Was worried for fear my guests would not bring enough liquor. Fears groundless. Didn't have to open a single bottle of my own. Food not bad but for next year must find a better phrase than "pot luck" for the invitations. Accepting six bean casseroles must be proof I am a good politician.

Note: Must learn to control my love of puns. Unnecessary to refer to those casseroles as has-beens. The only one who laughed was Dan Prosser and he thought I was talking about his wife.

Thursday January 2

No Council meeting last night. Just as well. No one in shape for debate. Must do something about Milky Becker. He is a good constable when it comes to summer traffic. Hardly a tourist gets through town without a ticket for something. Most mornings I find five, maybe ten dollars in my box at the post office, mailed back by some traveler with a conscience. Of course, I have to split it with Milky but that's only fair since he does all the chasing and all I do is have the tickets printed.

However, Milky gets kind of restless in winter. Maybe I'll give him an extra title. His family would like that. Come to think of it, every town should have a dog catcher. I don't know that there are more than three dogs around, but he could pick up each one once a year and charge, say, five dollars. Every little bit helps.

In any case, I've got to persuade Council to get him a proper uniform. And a proper cap. Upper Upsalquitch is getting too big for its policeman to be wearing one that says "Porter."

Friday January 3

Dan Prosser called. Wants me to go ice fishing tomorrow. You have to admire Dan. Anybody brave enough to sell used cars in a town this size and still take up the collection on Sunday is no coward. Just wish he wouldn't pick on me when he wants to go ice fishing. It has nothing to do with Dan. He sells his cars and his wife runs their general store. And ever since I got to be representative for Perpetual Life, they've been policy holders. Nice folk. But sitting out there in the cold plays hob with my posterior.

Told Dan that last year, so for Christmas he gave me a hot water bottle. But certainly didn't appreciate him presenting it to me at a Council meeting. Guess he thought he was being very funny. The way he went on about the piles I had sounded as if I was dipping my hand in the town till. And there was no way I could explain without someone wondering if I wasn't protesting too much. Rule One for a politician: don't say anything that provokes thought.

Saturday January 4

Gave in and went ice fishing over on Grog Brook. Didn't catch anything but at least had lots of time to think.

Found myself wondering if I am right for this job. I look at all the other people who might run for Mayor and can see good points in each. However, can also see that Upper Upsalquitch would suffer if it did not have a full-time Mayor. The town is still a long way from being able to offer a salary. And none of the others could afford to give all their time to it. So maybe, good or bad, I win by default, dear Brutus.

Could not have taken the job or kept it if I hadn't regarded myself as a professional right from the start. With me, being Mayor is a way of life. Would not want to be anything else. Nor, in truth, could I afford it right now.

The insurance business is great, but it hinges on my being Mayor. If I had to meet my bills on the insurance income from other sources it would be as awkward as wearing a rusty chastity belt.

Sunday January 5

In a town this small the Mayor simply has to go to church on Sunday. To make matters worse, you have to stay awake and look as though you're listening. Some Sundays my job seems hardly worth it.

More than that, you have to be careful because the minister secretly resents you. It's his show. When he finally winds it all up and goes to the door to be told how wonderful he was, there you are with a bunch of glad-handers grouped around you, blocking the way and stealing attention.

Don't know how to beat it. I have to be in church and I have to leave. I realize that the Reverend Angus has his own problem: he's not really shaking hands at the door, he's taking the congregation's pulse. About the only way he has of knowing whether it's safe to show up again next Sunday.

Monday January 6

Went into the Oriental Cafe today for coffee and to talk to proprietor Sim Jack about the Mayor's Picnic. You can't beat the Chinese for getting a new slant on things.

July 1st seems a long way off but in the Mayor business you've got to think ahead. Catch a guy early in snowy January and talk about a mid-summer picnic and you'd be surprised what he'll promise! Then all you have to do is keep reminding him until he feels he can't back out.

I know it's kind of mean to pick on poor old Sim. He's been around these parts quite a while, running his restaurant and the laundry next door. And he has always been mighty kind to me in the way of free coffee and food. After the first time, have never once had to mention that he operates without a license.

Today, sounded him out on my new idea. This year, I think we'll try an egg roll on the grass like I've read the Americans have at Easter at the White House.

Sim Jack baulked a bit. But he finally gave in, though he says it'll take him two days to make enough egg rolls for everyone.

Tuesday January 7

Spent today at home, shut up in my office getting ready for the weekly Council meeting at the school house tomorrow night. The first one of the year is always the toughest. This is when I give the troops the bad news on the budget.

Making Joe Azar the Treasurer was a smart move. It was a great day when I discovered that he is the one Councillor that has a little trouble with his multiplication. But that puts an extra load on me to keep the books balanced.

One thing I'd better do for sure is to get a little money for Annie Irving. Ever since old Casey cornered me into making her my secretary, she's been hinting that it wouldn't hurt to get paid. I'll bet if Casey had his daughter working in his bank, she wouldn't get anything. On payday he'd just show her his will. But I can see her side of it. She must have some expenses, even living at home. Not for cosmetics, that's for sure, but for all those movie magazines she's always carrying around. If she knew as much about the town's affairs as she does about the ones in Hollywood, she could be Mayor herself.

Wednesday January 8

As I expected, it was a rough meeting. Got Annie five dollars a week. Not much but a start. Establishing the precedent is always the hard part. After that, getting more is easy. It's a fundamental principle of democratic government.

Then there was a great ruckus over buying a new bench for the bus stop. I'd promised Bill Huggins earlier that the present one would be replaced. Folks like to sit outside his drug store and eat their lunch. Sim Jack objected because it hurts his restaurant business. Really had to bang my gavel to get it through.

To quieten things down, distributed a new pamphlet Perpetual Life has just sent me. Starts out slowly about Jesus feeding those thousands with five loaves and two fishes—then builds to a wallop asking what the multitude would have done if that bread and fish hadn't been available. Figure it's right on target for this town where most of the people are only interested in loafing and fishing.

Thursday January 9

Had a bright idea while shaving. A way to make Sim Jack feel better. Went to see him this morning and told him how in some cities benches are used for advertising. We would get Dusty Miller to paint "Eat at Sim Jack's" on the back of the bus stop bench. Sim was so pleased he almost smiled.

Then I visited Bill Huggins and told him what I had in mind. Bill, who gets an occasional free meal out of his fellow Councillor, got the message. But he couldn't resist suggesting that we change the wording to "Eat at the Oriental Cafe" so strangers wouldn't be set back by accidentally wandering next door into Sim's laundry. Good point. If Sim's kitchen was like his laundry, we'd all be long dead of the plague.

Friday January 10

Is there anything more invigorating than a cold, crisp winter day?

It was ten below when I got up this morning. Called Al Pines at *The Portent,* gave him a blast on dissolute youth so he'd have a quote for next week's front page, and went back to bed.

That's the way to enjoy this weather; get someone else stirred up and then watch through the bedroom window.

Annie called about ten. Said her father's car wouldn't start. Asked if there was anything she could do for me, if not she'd stay home. Fine by me. If there's one thing I learned from Grandpa Heber—and he said he learned it from his pa when they were still in the Boston states—it is to conserve your strength when you can against the day of need.

Over the years, I've worked pretty hard at it. I figure by now I am something of a conservation expert. When that day of need comes, I'm sure going to be ready for it!

While busy conserving, found myself wondering about Annie. Do you suppose the timid little brown mouse has ever met a rat? Have a feeling her timidity may be just a pose. If a man ever put a hand on her, she'd probably bare her teeth, growl like a tiger and, before he could escape, love him to death.

If it weren't for the pleasure her father would get out of my funeral, I might be tempted to try it.

Saturday January 11

Jim Dupuis, the Fire Chief, called to report that the pumper was frozen. Told him not to worry; being Saturday night, nobody will get hurt so long as it isn't the Legion Hall that's burning.

He certainly takes his job seriously. You can't burn leaves in your back yard anymore without Jim running up and yelling directions.

Dan Prosser got a barbecue last year but he had to give up using it. When Jim saw the smoke he showed up with the pumper and all the steaks turned out rare. So was some of the language.

Sunday January 12

Now that the long years of caring for Mother are over, I am able to stay in bed on Sunday mornings. Can linger until ten fifteen and still make it to church shaved and all. Of course, I don't get time to eat. But that old organ is so bad, a few rumbles from my pew are never noticed. Just wish I could wear my Romeo slippers. Getting my boots on and laced takes time. Strange how the older I get the more remote my feet seem!

Did appreciate the Prossers having me for lunch. The fish Dan caught. Very good. Usually we don't see much fish until summer. But since we don't allow camping or fishing within town limits, whenever I want some fish, Milky goes downstream until he finds a tourist with a catch. The town limits are fairly flexible.

Monday January 13

We had our first bank holdup in history today! Bank manager Casey Irving was just unlocking the door when two men walked up and pushed him inside.

Casey told them there was a time lock on the vault and they'd have to come back in an hour. They locked him in the john and left.

It was a pretty brave thing for Casey to do. First of all, he hasn't got a vault. Secondly, the safe he does have has a broken lock and hasn't been used for years.

Don't know where he keeps his money at night but I have a hunch the robbers were closer to it than they realized when they locked him up. I'm willing to bet that if you went into his john at night and flushed, the bank would go down the drain.

Tuesday January 14

The Upper Upsalquitch *Portent* brought out a special edition today, covering the attempted robbery. Al Pines made it sound big. A picture of Casey grinning determinedly and another of Constable Becker scratching his head.

So far, no clues as to who the men were or where they came from. Milky wants me to call in the Mounties but I think I'd better put that to a vote.

Wednesday January 15

As I suspected, the Council wants no part of the Mounties. Last time we had them in (when Dan Prosser's tractor was "stolen"—actually he'd forgotten he left it in his back hundred), they stayed a week and almost ate Sim Jack bankrupt. They asked some pretty embarrassing questions, too, like how it was that a town without a liquor store could get so tanked up on Saturday nights. We also had a little trouble with some of our females, but that's another story.

Called Milky after the meeting and told him we had faith in him. Oh boy!

Thursday January 16

Had a bright idea while shaving. I've never had a car. The Council doesn't feel we can afford one—and of course it's not the sort of thing a person would spend his *own* money on. But last night Annie and I were watching television and there was a big city funeral on. (Somebody's godfather, they said.) And there was this hearse, looking for all the world like a black stationwagon a mile long.

Thinking about it this morning, I suddenly realized that that hearse Fire Chief Dupuis keeps out back of his funeral parlor is getting pretty old. It would be a terrible thing if he was heading for the graveyard someday and the hearse died! If we could get one of those station wagon types, maybe the Council could rent it for my use between funerals.

Friday January 17

I certainly am disillusioned! Got a call from some man in Fredericton. Said he had just seen a story on our "attempted holdup."

After we talked a while, thanked him and went right over to see Casey Irving.

He admitted the truth: the man who telephoned me and another had come to the bank as Casey was opening up. But all they wanted was to cash a cheque. Casey told them the bank wasn't open (he hates cashing cheques—even for people who have accounts). They left and Casey went into the john (probably to count his money). The door jammed shut and he couldn't get out until the first depositor happened by. He was just too ashamed to admit it, so he lied.

Sure am glad we didn't call in the Mounties!

Saturday January 18

Tried out the new hearse idea on Jim Dupuis. He wasn't much
interested at first. Said he couldn't afford it. So I kept talking. Pretty
soon he began to get the picture. The point was he didn't *need*
money; the hearse would be free. That kind of got to him.

Casey Irving would lend the money and the Council would pay
enough rent to retire the loan.

"But suppose the Council won't go for it?" he says.

"Well," I replied, "that is a problem. But we'll just have to hope
that democracy will triumph. There are six councillors: now, you're
going to vote for it, and Casey will, because it's a nice, safe loan. And
I imagine we can count on Dan Prosser being for it, seeing as how he's
the car dealer involved. So the worst we can have is a tie. And then
I, as Mayor, will cast the deciding vote."

Sunday January 19

Have been trying to find out who it was that let Casey out of the john.
It isn't idle curiosity. When you're up against a man like him, you
need all the ammunition you can get. Sort of poked around on it with
Annie but apparently her father hasn't said much at home.

Dropped by Letty Hinch's yesterday morning. Our only seamstress
has a knack for putting things together. Her place is a clearing-house
for anything our womenfolk have on their minds; the town bitching
post.

Naturally, I swore her to secrecy before letting her in on what the
"robbery" was really all about. From the way that people smiled when
Casey came into church today, I could tell I had brought a little
sunshine into her old maid's heart. I hope that, in exchange, she gets
me that name.

Monday January 20

Today's issue was law and order. Editor Al Pines, having made a big thing of the bank "robbery," is putting the heat on me to know why we aren't trying harder to catch the criminals. Sometimes it gets so you don't know which lie to tell.

If I give him a statement saying we're making progress and then it comes out that it was only old Casey stuck in the can, I'll look bad. If I say "No progress," I'll still look bad.

The one thing I can't do is give Al the truth. If I do Casey will be embarrassed—and roaring mad at me. And getting re-elected without the support of your banker is like trying to climb Mount Everest without a rope; you may be able to do it, but it has never been done before.

Tuesday January 21

The problem with being largely self-educated is that my head is a pickle barrel of unrelated facts. Example: there is no way I can be a better Mayor, insurance man or money-maker because I know that this is Saint Agnes' Day (Latin: Agnus Dei).

Poor Agnes! She should have taken it on the lam. Just because she refused to marry a pagan, they treated her rather badly. She was whipped and put on the rack (hence "rack of lamb") and then they tried to burn her at the stake. She didn't burn too well, so they chopped off her head—which was kind of conclusive. He certainly must have been an ugly pagan!

Remember reading the John Keats poem about her in school. The lines about how she "Unclasps her warmed jewels one by one; Loosens her fragrant bodice; by degrees Her rich attire creeps rustling to her knees." That was the closest thing to pornography we had going for us in those gentle days.

Now the books and movies are so explicit they take all the fun out of discovering things for yourself. Sometimes yearn for that period between when Adam ate the apple and Washington eliminated the cherry. But I guess life is a bit like a contour sheet; there's no turning back.

11

Wednesday January 22

Had a little trouble with the vote on the new hearse. But once Jim Dupuis assured them that the black side curtains would not be on it when I was driving, things settled down.

Clare Latrouche was kind of sassy until I gave her the hard eye. She's pretty proud of being the only woman Councillor in these parts and maybe it crossed her mind that since I pretty well pick who's going to run around here, she had better shut up. In fact, she more than shut up, she voted for the rental. Which was great since it saved me having to vote.

Thursday January 23

The annual library grant from the Carnegie Foundation came today. Rushed over to get Joe Azar to endorse it so that I could get it into the bank. It was late this year and I was beginning to worry. The bills were starting to pile up.

Next step is to write the annual thank-you letter and get Letty Hinch, as Town Librarian, to sign it. This time I think I'll try to put in a tactful sentence suggesting they get their cheques to us sooner. Christmas is an awfully expensive time of year.

Don't want to hurt their feelings or upset them though; they're good folks. One of these days, as a tribute to them, I think we should set up a real library. That shelf in Bill Huggins' drug store is getting kind of full.

Friday January 24

Called Bill Ellis, the school principal, this morning and said I thought it was time the school had a television set so the kids could see some of those educational programs I'm paying for with my income tax. Said I'd like to give them mine—as a gift. He was most appreciative. After a little discussion, we agreed that since it wasn't costing the school anything, the amount on the receipt he'll give me for tax purposes doesn't matter. Seemed a little surprised though when I told him the figure I had in mind. I guess he didn't realize how much a new set with colour is going to cost me.

Saturday January 25

Annie stayed on after work tonight to cook for me. In the sitting-room afterwards, we talked for a long while. At one point she asked me why I had decided to run for Mayor in the first place. Then she fell asleep before I could finish my answer. Just like a woman!

Left me awake and thinking. Surprised to realize I can't remember when I decided. Some people seem to know early that they're going to be doctors or lawyers. I guess I just took a look at the jobs in town and picked out Mayor for mine.

Didn't get it right off, of course. People here don't like a Mayor that's too young. So I went in the insurance business first. Can't think of a better way of getting to know other people's affairs—unless it's by doing their laundry.

Sunday January 26

Didn't know quite what to do last night after Annie fell asleep in that chair. Kind of nice, the two of us sitting there. Like it used to be before Mother died; a long evening with a woman in the room. But Mother didn't have Casey Irving for a father.

Casey has always had it in for me. Thinks all the money in town should come to him. Watches me like a hawker, waiting for a chance to catch me out. That's why, when I told Council I wanted a secretary (there was a cute little Indian girl I had in mind), he jumped in to support me and then offered Annie's services free. The Council accepted on the spot.

So there sat the Mata Hari of Upper Upsalquitch, her legs apart, her head back, snoring her little heart out. And all I could do was look.

Along about eleven I turned on the TV to get the news and she woke up and went home. She sure is a nice girl! Pity her old man is so narrow. For a banker, he certainly is opposed to change.

Monday January 27

Went to see Letty Hinch today about her insurance. Her twenty year endowment is about paid up. Just wanted to be very sure, for her sake, that she wasn't planning to take it all in cash. Persuaded her to buy a paid up straight life with it, convertible to pension if she needs it later.

It's kind of delicate work, talking to an old maid about her future! Got my face slapped by one old girl years ago. Later, she married a widowed farmer and they both ended up customers. She bought a small straight life (what we call our "lay away plan"—just enough for the funeral). He bought a pretty decent policy, naming her as the beneficiary. Six weeks later he was dead of over-exertion and she was off to Florida.

Tuesday January 28

Had another one of those nuisance letters from Perpetual Life. Every now and then some "expert" gets all steamed up about efficiency. In comes a letter saying my policy holders are too slow in paying their premiums. This is simply not so. People around here are very honest and very prompt. They get their monthly payments in to me right on the dot (unless they're ill or something; then they know I'll cover for them for a month and only charge them 2%).

Every payment I get goes into the bank right away. And when their annual payment is due, the money is ready and waiting in my savings account and off goes a cheque to the company. The only time there's any delay is when there's an interest payment on my savings account coming up.

Wednesday January 29

Having my office right in the house has its pros and cons. On a cold, stormy day like this one has been, the pros come on pretty strong.

Figured Annie would never make it, so didn't bother to get dressed. Consequence was she caught me in my quilted bathrobe and in the embarrassing position of being on my knees under the desk and crying, "Wherefore art thou, Romeos?" She fished out the slippers I was looking for and I retreated to the bedroom to put on more suitable attire. In my case, it takes a while to suit a tire, so by the time I returned to the office she had a cup of coffee waiting for each of us, had removed my cereal bowl from atop the minute book and was busy filing the tax receipts. (We never send the receipts to the tax-payers; just keep them here in case somebody wants one. Saves postage.)

Good girl, Annie. Am beginning to wonder if she doesn't sort of like me. Not that I want to get involved with a woman at my age. But I'd sure like to have a warm body around the house.

Thursday January 30

Snowstorm blew itself out during the night. Dumped a lot of snow.
Dusty Miller didn't get to shovelling the walk until ten and I was a
little miffed. Since we don't have a city hall, people tend to drop in
to my place with their problems. That's why I've always insisted on
the town street-cleaner, namely Dusty, keeping my walk and driveway
cleared. After all, if they're going to pay for the use of my front
parlor as the Mayor's office, they've got a duty to keep it accessible.

Dusty's kind of a hard man to reprimand, though. Always agreeing
with you. You tell him he's late, he says, "I sure am!" You tell him
he's not making the path wide enough, he nods and says, "I'm sure
not." But he never comes any earlier—or makes the path any wider.
If he keeps it up, we may run him for parliament.

Friday January 31

The new colour TV set arrived this morning. I had them take it
around to the back and uncrate it there. No point in making my
neighbours jealous. Got them to pile the crating in the garage; will sell
it for kindling.

It's a fine set. In these parts, you don't need all those channel
numbers, with only two stations available.

When Annie arrived she was delighted. Seems she's quite a TV
fan. She got so carried away she ended up frying some food for us
and we ate it in front of the set. It's amazing how different people
look in colour! She likes the Prime Minister greener than I do.

Saturday February 1

Hope I don't get in trouble with Casey Irving. Couple of weeks ago I sent away to Antigonish for some literature on the credit union idea. Pretty interesting. Just like a bank, except you don't need any money of your own to start one. All the depositors are shareholders (one vote each) and they put up the money by making regular deposits.

It would knock hell out of Casey's bank. There isn't a person in town doesn't envy Casey his money. Give them the offer that for switching their accounts they become shareholders and get a piece of the action and I think they'd all move—and fast.

Only thing I haven't figured out yet is how *I* make a buck. They don't spell that out. Seeing that the material was printed by a university, I guess that's not too unnatural: universities are prophet-oriented.

Sunday February 2

One of the key differences between people in the north and south on this continent relates to the weather. Am always reading about how people down there get riled up in the long hot summer. In our parts it's the winter that gets them. A town like ours becomes shut in on itself after snowfall. There's nothing much to do and not much fun in doing it.

Since we don't boast a cocktail lounge or even a hotel with a bar, you drink in the home or you go down to the Legion Hall and bull your way through two world wars for a few beers. Saturday nights are the big nights at the Legion.

Apparently the frustrations of winter began to get to some of the boys last night and they got pretty loaded. Someone spread the word that Sim Jack was a Communist spy. We don't have Ku Klux Klanners up here, but some of our guys can be as bad when they get a few sheets in the wind.

Off they went to find Sim. He was working late in his laundry, heard them coming and locked the door. When they tried to break in, he let them have it with the drain hose from his tubs. Those that weren't already sloshed felt it most.

Monday February 3

Up in Montreal today someone put a bomb in a mailbox and set off the media. Television tonight was full of it. The boys in Québec do make it hard to maintain national unity!

We Canadians are basically an insecure lot anyway. I hear ours is the only country whose national airline gives in-flight swimming lessons.

Tuesday February 4

Annie says I really must do something about my clothes. She says I am not very up to date, and outside Madame Tussaud's I'm the only man still wearing plus-fours.

I like them. I've had them for years and would miss them. They have all of the advantages of the kilt without any of the potential embarrassment.

Wednesday February 5

At Council Meeting tonight, we all congratulated Councillor Jack
on his smart handling of the Legion boys Saturday night.

Since Sim is the only Oriental in town (and the only one I have
ever known), I have no one to compare him with but it seems to me
that if all Chinese are as smart as he is, then maybe we *should* be
worrying more about the Chinese communists!

Thursday February 6

Annie is becoming a major factor in my life. When she tidies up the
office, it's great. I am not a tidy person. When she stays on to see I
get a decent meal, it's wonderful. But the last few days she's taken
to getting into things that are none of her business. Like my plus-fours
(or, as she calls them, "knickers").

Last night she stayed to watch TV. And somewhere along in the
evening she must have slipped into my bedroom and hidden them.
This morning couldn't find them anywhere. Had to wear trousers
down to Sim Jack's. Everybody stared at me.

Finally found them when I got back. She had put them in the
broom closet, under the carpet sweeper, a place I haven't looked
for years.

When she returned from lunch I had them on. Neither one of us
said anything, though she did sort of sniff. I have a feeling that the
battle isn't over. Perhaps I'd better keep them under my mattress
with my income tax returns.

It's getting so there's nothing sacred anymore.

Friday February 7

Met Father Ignatius LaPierre on the street today and hauled him into Sim Jack's for coffee. (Sim's always good about that. If he sees someone is my guest, he refuses to charge them either.) Told the Father about my interest in credit unions. He got quite excited. Knows all about them. Took a course in how to set them up, he says.

As delicately as possible, brought up the question of how you make money out of them. He looked shocked. "But they're cooperative!" he said, as if he was quoting Scripture. "You don't make profits. In a credit union, everyone is equal."

"Everyone?" I said, feeling kind of ill at the thought. He nodded.

Well, there goes another nick in my gun as far as his church is concerned.

Saturday February 8

Was pleased to find that *The Portent* this week carried my latest letter. Al, bless him, even put it in a box!
Dear Ed.,

As Mayor I feel it my duty to draw to the attention of our citizens through your pages the deplorable conditions which face us when we walk down Main Street on a Sunday morning.

In a town of this size we cannot afford—except at the price of higher taxes—a street cleaning department. This means that each of us must do his part to keep our town tidy. During most of the week I must confess that we are pretty good at it. The prevailing wind from Québec also helps.

But for some reason we lose our reason on Saturday night. This is especially evident in the area surrounding the Legion Hall. Scraps of brown wrapping paper shaped suspiciously like wine bottles, old cardboard boxes, cigarette cartons, bottle caps and sundry other items of debris abound.

I was especially embarrassed last Sunday morning when I spied a shoe sticking out of the entrance to an alley. As a good citizen I assayed to kick it into the gutter, only to find to my dismay that there was still a foot in it, the owner of which roused himself sufficiently to address me in rather improper language.

Sunday February 9

The choir sang one of my favourites today; the old Scottish Psalter version of the Twenty-third Psalm. When the Reverend Angus took over to deliver his sermon, my mind wandered back to it. ". . . In pastures green/He leadeth me/The quiet waters by. . . ."

We don't have much in the way of pastures around here, but there are spots where the river is reasonably quiet.

Many people think that Upper Upsalquitch is up the Upsalquitch. It isn't, it's down. That is, if you're looking at it from Upsalquitch. But that's ironic, since we look down on Upsalquitch.

Always have. Admittedly, Upsalquitch has a butcher, a baker, a doctor and a dentist and we don't. But *we* have quality. That's why we call our town "Upper" even though it's down river.

Anyway, the Upsalquitch flows north—until it joins the Restigouche. Funny, you keep hearing about how famous salmon from there is. It's on menus in New York, they tell me. The truth is, that's *Upsalquitch* salmon that just happened to be passing through, but I guess we'll never get the credit.

Monday February 10

We had an odd sight this morning; an airplane towing a banner that said "Vive Québec Libre."

Our problem here in Upper Upsalquitch is that any talk of a "Free Québec" only reminds us of how much Québec has already had free. Perhaps we're a mite touchy about it, being Maritimers. When the country was getting itself confederated, we supplied the free booze and boat rides for the delegates. And all we got out of it were some broken promises and a feeling of lonesomeness. But we're still Canadians.

Another thing: a lot of the folks in New Brunswick here are just as good French as there are anywhere. In these parts, it's what you are, not what you were that counts.

Tuesday February 11

Walking down to Sim Jack's this morning it struck me that the tourists and fishermen that pass through may think it odd that we don't have names for our streets. Guess it's because we all know where we live.

Stopped off to see Al Pines. He has some big type he uses for auction posters and scarlet fever signs. Agreed to set "Main Street," "Back Road" and "Grog Brook Road." Will get Dusty to stick them up and see what happens. If no one objects, I may be able to make a deal with some city that has spare signs. It might be kind of nice to be living on Pennsylvania Avenue.

Abraham Lincoln's Birthday

Wednesday February 12

Even though there are no Americans living in Upper Upsalquitch, we are not averse to recognizing that they do exist.

I drew to the attention of Council tonight that today is the birthday of President Lincoln.

They got all enthused for some reason. Before I could stop them, they rammed through a motion that I send him a "Happy Birthday" telegram.

Getting that off the Minutes book took a little tact!

Thursday February 13

I don't know what it is that Annie holds against my plus-fours. She was at me again today. It's not as though they're worn or rumpled or anything. After all, I put them under my mattress every night.

I wonder if she's trying to put me into bright yellow golf slacks or something like that? Being Mayor is close enough to being the Town Clown without wearing funny pants.

Valentine's Day

Friday February 14

I suppose it was too much to expect. But did find myself wishing while shaving that somebody would think to send the Mayor a Valentine.

None appeared. Not even a nasty one. Last year, at least got one of those slipped under my door. Written in a childish hand, it read

To our Mayor.
He's so unfair
Sometimes we wish
He wasn't there!

Not very encouraging. (Bad drawing, too. Or do I really look like Punch?) Would have preferred it to read:

To our beloved and sterling Mayor
Who works so hard and is so fair.
Please find enclosed a little cheque
To prove that we all give a heck.

But I guess it showed that someone cared enough to send the very worst. In this business, it's not the jeering but the silences that get you.

Saturday February 15

Donna Reed! It came to me as Annie and I were watching television that perhaps there actually is such a person.

For years, whenever someone pointed to a young female on TV and asked "Who's that?" I have said "That? Oh, that's Donna Reed." They all look the same.

The worst that has ever happened is that if the girl is correctly identified by someone else I have had to say firmly, "Well, she *looks* like Donna Reed!" No one has ever been able to deny that I was right.

Sunday February 16

Poking around in a closet today found an old cake of soap. The brand Mother used to use. Don't know how it got there. Doesn't say much for the way I kept house after she took to her wheelchair!

Wrapped the cake in wax paper and put it away carefully. Sometime it may be valuable as an antique. People are collecting everything else these days, so why not?

Especially a brand like that. *Fairy Soap*. Their advertising used to ask "Is there a little Fairy in your home?" I presume they got laughed out of business.

That's one thing we're out of tune with in Upper Upsalquitch: the amount of attention being paid today to the homosexual. There was one man out on Grog Brook Road that I used to think might qualify. Walked with a sort of mincing step. Turned out he had a hernia.

Monday February 17

Every now and then I try to write a guest editorial for Al Pines.
It gives him a break and reminds the voters who their Mayor is.

Groping for a topic for this week's edition, wondered if I couldn't
do a piece headed "Pollution Is Good For You." It's easy for an
Upper Upsalquitchian not to worry about pollution. All we have to
do is stay out of Upsalquitch. Apparently the rest of the world is up
to its drears in garbage.

Despite all of the concern expressed, I've been forced to a simple
conclusion: since I do not believe that mankind is going to drown in
its own refuse, then it must be true that we will adapt. Those who
adapt best will become the dominant strain and those who are least
exposed will be the first to go under. Pollution is only a phase of
evolution.

Called Al and discussed the idea with him. He kind of liked it but
pointed out that perhaps it would not sit too well with some of the
readers. They might reason that since Upper Upsalquitch is relatively
pollution-free, the Mayor is forecasting their doom.

That doesn't exactly fit in with my purpose in writing editorials so
I've scrapped my notes. But still think my idea is right.

Tuesday February 18

Must get over soon to see the dentist. That left molar is at it again.
Most of the time you don't mind that we don't have a dentist or a
doctor here, but sometimes it's inconvenient. Not a very balanced
town, really.

Example: most towns have a service club or two. Rotary, Kiwanis,
that sort of thing. Guess we're short on joiners. For those who like to
get together all we have is the Town Council. And it's not easy to
become a member of it. Once on it, people don't resign and the
public doesn't push much for change.

You do have the occasional upset. Like when Madame Latrouche
gets all heated up about Women's Lib and tries to bully her way
through. But mostly it's like a club where everyone knows everyone
else's business and helps them mind it.

Wednesday February 19

Freedom of speech is a sacred right which must be defended at all costs.

As I said to Dan Prosser at Council Meeting tonight, "I disapprove of what you say and I will defend to the death my right to tell you so."

One of the ways free speech can best be protected is by knowing when to tell someone who is abusing it to shut up.

There is, to me, a big difference between free speech and free wheeling. Besides, Dan was wrong. Calling for bids on the new street lights would just be a waste of time. I've already placed the order.

Thursday February 20

Read about a wonderful idea in a Miama paper that a tourist left here last year: termite insurance.

Seems that termites are so bad in some places down south and out in California that people buy insurance against them.

Phoned Dusty Miller and asked him if he had ever seen any in these parts. He said none that he'd recognize. I told him to keep his eyes open. As soon as I can get a copy of one of those U.S. policies and find out what they charge, I've a feeling we're going to start seeing termites all over the place.

Friday February 21

The car has finally come! Dan Prosser called me and Jim Dupuis over to see it. It certainly is a beautiful thing. Must admit I didn't expect it to look quite *so* much like a hearse. The one seat in the front and the rollers on the back floor sort of give it away. But it's not the fluted chrome window posts so much as the black vine leaves that bother me. Anyway, it's a car—and mine to drive!

Jim wanted to take it home to show the family, but I felt it proper, as Mayor, to remind him of his legal commitment. He didn't have a funeral today, so the car was for me. (The way he looked at me for a minute I thought maybe we *were* going to have a funeral.) But he is an honest man and had to admit I was right. Can hardly wait to show it to Annie.

George Washington's Birthday

Saturday February 22

Looking back, I can see there might have been a better way of introducing Annie to the new car than to spring it on her as a complete surprise. Women are funny.

She had gone over to visit her Uncle Casper, who is getting on and has been ill in bed for some time. So I drove over to see her. I was so excited that I guess I came down the street at a pretty good clip. The tires kind of screamed when I braked in front of their place. Going up the steps, I noticed the neighbours coming out of their doors and hurrying over. But if I thought anything, it was that they wanted to have a look at the car.

That's why I was completely surprised when Annie, opening the door and seeing me with the neighbours behind me—and then, over our shoulders, a hearse—fainted dead away.

Sunday February 23

Yesterday was George Washington's birthday. Not being a man to pass up an opportunity like that, the Reverend Angus today devoted his sermon to "What Is Truth?" All about young George and the cherry tree.

He quoted that poet lady Emily Dickinson who wrote, "Truth is as old as God." I guess just as we don't understand God, so we really don't understand truth. But it isn't for lack of trying. The Reverend sure did *his* best today.

We ranged from jesting Pilate to Mark Twain. In between, we got sprinkled with more drops of poetry than have hit me in a long while.

But he never did explain what George had against cherry trees.

Monday February 24

Read an article this afternoon on how well Japan is doing in selling things to the world. Seems like this might be one answer to our fear of U.S. domination here in Canada. The only thing is, if the Japanese industries are U.S. controlled, should I learn to speak Japanese or skip that step and concentrate on learning American?

Tuesday February 25

Got two envelopes from the federal government today. The kind with
a hole in them so your name shows through. Naturally, you have to
open them. (I figured if they had to write to me twice on the same
day, the jig must really be up.) Inside each envelope was a plain piece
of paper with my name and address on it. Enclosed was another slip
that said "Help Fight Inflation! Keep Costs Down!"

At first, I thought that someone was trying to put one over on me.
But then I found everyone had gotten them. A die-cut envelope, two
sheets of paper, a personal-addressing process, a printing job, a
collating and inserting job—and the Post Office's cost of mailing to
millions of households. Just to tell us to keep costs down. That's
like swallowing a diamond to see how well your bowels work.

Wednesday February 26

Following hard on the heels of those two envelopes from Ottawa
yesterday, darned if today's mail didn't bring my Income Tax forms
—weeks late this year, but I'd be the last to rush them. It's always a
saddening moment when they come, like getting the news of the loss
of a friend. I've been filling out those silly forms for years now—and
I suppose that someday I'll actually have to pay money—but every
time I do it, I find myself wishing that there were some easier way to
raise tax funds. It's not right for the government to be so nosey.

Thursday February 27

At Council Meeting last night, Madame Latrouche said that maybe what Upper Upsalquitch needed was a Town Income Tax. She says New York City has one and it works real well.

I asked her what we would do with the money and she came up with a pretty good answer: "Pay the councillors salaries."

Must say the other councillors perked up a bit at that idea. Showed more interest in the proceedings than they have since the night Letty Hinch tried to get *Peyton Place* banned from the library by reading us the good parts.

A Mayor has to be a sort of father to his council. Right away—before they could do something foolish—I called for a committee to look into it. That takes care of that for awhile and, if this committee is like most, forever.

Friday February 28

Had a visit from Madame Latrouche. Apparently, she sensed Wednesday night that I didn't think her Town Income Tax was the greatest thing ever.

It's interesting. If a man comes to see you and plunks himself down in a chair, there are a dozen different ways of getting him back on his feet and on his way. But when a woman sits she stays sat until she herself wants to stand. It must have something to do with the nesting instinct.

After Madame Latrouche had said her piece (and I had lied through my teeth), she still wouldn't budge. I tried everything (the cough, the glance at the watch . . .). Finally in desperation I said, "I wonder if the varnish on that chair is dry yet?" That got her up in a hurry. From there, it was easy to talk her to the door.

Saturday March 1

Today is St. David's Day—everywhere else except in Upper Upsalquitch where, lacking anyone with the proper antecedents, we have welshed on it.

That ruckus last week over the car is all behind us now. Annie has recovered and forgiven me. We went driving today.

She seemed sort of reluctant to get in it. (Some women are like that about cars.) But once inside she relaxed completely; slumped right down on the floor. Out in the country, she perked up a bit though and looked out the windows.

I'm grateful we're not courting. When it comes to a car for necking, I could think of a more comfortable model than one with rollers on the floor.

Sunday March 2

Sermon today was on the Golden Rule. The Reverend Angus was in good form, which is more than I can say for the choir. As a matter of fact, if anyone ever took the Golden Rule seriously anymore, can you imagine what would happen?

The congregation would hold a secret meeting and then, on a given Sunday, after the choir has rended its anthem, the congregation would stand up and sing it back at them. And the choir, for a change, would have to sit there and take it, the way we do every Sunday.

Monday March 3

Monday is sort of a dark day in the Mayor business. People tend to run down as the week wears on. And one of the things they run down is the Mayor.

This means that Monday's mail has a high abuse level. And while I'm reading it the phone usually starts to crackle as someone who has had to spend his weekend at home with his wife takes it out on me.

Annie says it's all part of the job. Which seems to be true. I've talked to a few other mayors and they seem to take it for granted— even though some of them run into much higher levels than I do. In fact, I have noted that the ones from larger cities get proportionately more abuse.

Tuesday March 4

I think I've devised an equation to calculate "The Mayor's Abuse Level" or simply "MAL" (it's good Canadian thinking to have bilingual acronyms.) Here's how it looks:

$$L = A \frac{P}{3} \times 100$$

Thus, the Level (L) is an index of the local Abuse (A) multiplied by the population (P) expressed as a percentage of three million (which is an arbitrary figure). This index (L) can then be used by all mayors on a comparative basis. If, for example, someone says I'm doing a bad job, I know I'm getting (L).

Wednesday March 5

Debated whether I should try out my MAL idea on the boys at Council tonight. Decided against it since they're all major contributors to the Abuse Level. Found myself looking around the room tonight and referring to them all in my mind as my MAL-contents.

Nothing major on the agenda. Milky Becker sent in word that his uniform trousers need replacing. I ruled he should try and make do until warm weather. Then we'll get the legs cut off and he can wear shorts for the summer.

Adjourned at nine p.m. to Sim Jack's for coffee. Not unnaturally, the conversation turned once again to pollution.

Thursday March 6

Dropped in to see Bill Huggins at the drug store this morning. Accepted his kind offer of a milkshake. Real purpose was to see how my books were selling. Bill and I have a little deal going. I see to it that the drug store stays the only place in town where the kids can buy their schoolbooks. Bill, in turn, keeps an eye on the kids who drop in on their way home from school. If he sees one of them carrying a book that looks a little ragged, he gives the kid a new one and puts it on the parents' account. Over the school year this racks up a surprising number of extra sales. And since I get ten per cent on all books sold, I'm really proud of how well-equipped our students are.

Friday March 7

Casey has decided that Annie had better get married. Being Casey, he has gone out and found a good deal for her. A widower in Boiestown who, oddly enough, also happens to be a banker.

Old Captain Morganic has been planning all this behind her back. Now, she's confronted with a fate worse than death: a *fait accompli*.

We spent most of the afternoon today talking about it. Annie has nothing against marriage. In fact, I think that at her age she's willing to marry anything that twitches—so long as she gets to pick it for herself. What gets her back up is that her father says it's all arranged, and she hasn't met the lucky man yet. He's supposed to hit town tomorrow afternoon. "He may not be all that bad," I pointed out. "Why don't you wait and see?"

Annie looked at me a little oddly and said, "But I thought I had to cook dinner for you tomorrow night." I've got some heavy thinking to do.

Saturday March 8

It looked like it was going to be a long day when I got up. Sort of moped around the house until noon. Didn't feel like doing much of anything. Then the phone rang. It was Annie.

"Should I still come over and cook dinner?" she asked.

"What happened to your suitor?"

"I—I'd rather wait and tell you when I see you," she said quietly.

Turned out, as she explained it over dinner, that her father's choice had changed his mind. I gather Annie didn't feel very flattered.

"Being rejected before he'd even met me doesn't seem very fair," she complained.

"Well," I said, feeling somehow very happy about it, "I'll bet your father was mad."

"Was he ever!" said Annie. "Especially since the old goat called collect!"

Sunday March 9

Saw Annie in church today. She always sits way over on the other side. We never say much, just nod politely to each other. This morning, I nodded as usual. But she sort of flounced around and cut me dead. It was kind of embarrassing. I hope no one noticed.

Trouble was I didn't know what upset her. We had a great chat and a good dinner last night. Watched a bit of the hockey game. Then she got up and yawned and said she guessed she'd better be going. I said fine, and she went and got her coat and stood around for a minute kind of uncertain and then went out, slamming the door.

Damn all women anyway! They blame men for everything. If it weren't for us where would they be? But little thanks we get! God would have been smart to have created a third sex, so we would both have someone to pick on.

Monday March 10

Today's mail brought me that termite insurance policy I sent to Miami for. The rates seem a little high for these parts. But if a fellow wants to have his home protected he has to expect to pay for it.

Took the policy to Al Pines at the paper and had a hundred copies made. Talked to Dusty Miller some about termites. Since he's never seen one he's coming over to the house in the morning so I can show him the pictures in the encyclopedia. I figure if he's going to be appointed the town's Termite Inspector, I'd better invest a little time in teaching him what to inspect for.

Tuesday March 11

I'm not too sure Dusty buys the termite deal. Showed him the pictures. Read to him about how they eat right through posts and can bring a whole house tumbling down. All he kept saying was, "Well, it ain't happened yet!"

Explained to him that that was what insurance was all about. Tried the old joke on him about the guy in New York City who has discovered how to protect himself from tigers. He just claps his hands. He's been wandering around Manhattan clapping his hands for ten years and hasn't been bitten yet. "See?" I concluded. "This insurance is just like the guy clapping hands."

"Umph," said Dusty, "Sounds like a lot of clap to me!"

Wednesday March 12

At tonight's meeting, Father LaPierre came by to request permssion to hold Mass at the movie house between features on Sundays. It was unfortunate that Councillor Huggins, who has the pop and popcorn concession at the theatre, was not absent. I had to bang my gavel to drown out some of his language.

Couldn't understand his objection. After all, it isn't as if it were Communion.

Discussed the idea of street signs. Not much support. Clare Latrouche said if all I was worried about was the tourists, we only needed two signs: "In" and "Out."

Thursday March 13

The guy that wrote the song "Ah, Sweet Mystery of Life!" should have put his other foot in it and written "Ah, Sweet Mystery of Woman!"

Here it is almost a week since Annie announced on one day that she had a problem and on the next that she had the solution. Since then she's hardly spoken to me except on business. Even when I gave her a really interesting policy to type up, she didn't say "Thanks." (For some reason, she usually likes typing policies. Seems to regard it as a bonus for being the Mayor's secretary, bless her heart.)

Anyway, I think I'll make a special effort to be nice to her tomorrow. If that doesn't work, I may have to use alternate means.

Friday March 14

Annie came bursting in the door all warmth and smiles this morning. What gets in to a woman that makes her change like that overnight? Sort of caught me off base because I'd been rehearsing all the nice things I was going to say to her. Sure hate to waste a rehearsal!

Well, it wasn't *all* waste. She made dinner for me tonight and then we settled down for an evening together just like before. I said a few nice things, but I have a feeling I have to be a little cautious. I may be about to be caught in an Irving pincer movement.

Saturday March 15

Dusty Miller came around today to tidy up outside. The snow always leaves a mess behind when it goes and it's not in the best interests of Upper Upsalquitch for the Mayor's residence to look untidy.

Unfortunately, it started to rain just after he got here, so I invited him in. Said, "Since your time is paid for anyway, Dusty, I suppose you'd rather be working." He agreed. So to make him feel better about taking the town's money I took him down in the cellar and put him to tidying it up. Annie came in with my groceries at noon and made him a sandwich. He was doing such a good job I didn't have the heart to tell him it had stopped raining just after he went downstairs.

Sunday March 16

I have always been fascinated by religion as a business. When I sit in church and watch the Reverend Angus perform, I find myself wondering how it is that with such a great story to tell, they don't make more money. Bad management at the top, I suspect.

I do know one thing: every time the Reverend lets himself go on Hell versus Heaven, I get a phone call the next day from some old geezer who is suddenly a little more conscious of the hereafter and wants to fatten up his policies before it's too late.

Today's sermon was on the Good Samaritan. That's on the beam, too, but a little subtle.

Monday March 17

Not many green ties show up in Upper Upsalquitch. Too many Orangemen. Did think one time of making more of an event out of it. Read somewhere that over in Chicago on this day they colour the river green. That'd be no problem here: the Upsalquitch already is. Council discouraged me from planning a parade or anything. In fact, it was one of the few times that Casey was my only supporter. Guess that's because green is his favourite colour.

Had an idea when I was shaving this morning. Thinking back to yesterday, why not suggest to Al Pines that he publish the Reverend Angus' sermons? If *The Portent* would carry them it would help a lot of people, including me. They wouldn't have to carry all of them, of course. Just the real stingers. And maybe Father Ignatius has some on the "you can't take it with you" theme also. (Some of my best policy holders are Catholics.) It would be a real public service.

Tuesday March 18

I make mistakes. This hard fact hit me between the eyes this morning. It happened that when I went into Sim Jack's, Al Pines was already there. I was so fired up with the idea of getting him to print sermons on the shortness of life I didn't notice he was still long on coffee.

Should have waited for that moment of quiet despair at the end of the first cup: you sit there thinking that as long as you live you will never have another drop of Sim's brew—which only goes from bitter to worse. And all the while out of the corner of your eye, you can see him coming closer and closer with that black pot. And you know that when he fills your cup again you will actually thank him for it.

I have learned a great lesson: never hit a man with an idea when he is down in the mouth.

Wednesday March 19

Got Dusty Miller made Termite Inspector at Council meeting tonight. Wasn't hard once I assured our elected representatives that we wouldn't have to pay him for the honour. He goes looking for termites and if he finds any the homeowner pays him for the job of exterminating them.

I figure if Dusty ever does find any there'll be a government pamphlet available to tell him what to do. God knows, there are pamphlets on everything else! (The most accurate title I ever saw was one one marked "Types of Hog Wash.")

I didn't mention a word about insurance tonight. Let the idea spread that we have an inspector first. People will figure an inspector must have something to inspect. Then we'll act.

Thursday March 20

At 2:08 p.m. Spring began, or so Letty Hinch informed me on the telephone. There was so much static on the line, had difficulty hearing her. The Bell people should certainly do something. Every time we get a snowstorm the telephones start jingling on their own and reception reminds you of the early crystal-set days of radio.

The condition has its blessing of course. The beginning of Spring may be the greatest event of the year to Letty. But I can take it quite calmly and if it hadn't been for the static I would have been hard put to give the topic the length of attention she seemed to think it demanded.

I hate to think how long she will go on the day she discovers sex.

Friday March 21

Al Pines ran a piece in *The Portent* on Dusty being made Termite Inspector. Treated it quite properly although I did wonder why, just below the item, he quoted a short poem:

> Some ancient termite knocked on wood
> And tasted it, and thought it good,
> So that is why your Auntie Fay
> Went through the floor the other day.

There are times when I wonder whether Al takes his responsibilities as an editor seriously enough.

I can only hope his readers took the lines as a warning.

Saturday March 22

This afternoon, had a visit from Ned Dervish. I figured he hadn't just come to sit a spell. He had his matinee going at the movie house and Ned usually is right there while the lights are out. (He says it's to keep order, but I think he likes to watch what's going on in the back rows.)

After some hemming and hawing he got to the point. There's a federal election coming up and he'd been asked to see if I wanted to run.

Well, it didn't take long for me to answer. I'd thought *that* through years ago. There's no way you'd get me to move to Ottawa. They're nothing but a bunch of crooks up there. Every one of them is out to get everything he can for himself.

Down here, it's different. I have the field pretty much to myself.

Sunday March 23

There's something funny going on, and I think I know what it is. After church today, standing around outside talking for a while as we do, Casey Irving came up to me and said sort of tentative like, "I hear Ned Dervish was in to see you yesterday." I nodded and waited. "Well," he says, "I just want you to know how delighted I am with your decision. You are the best mayor we've ever had and it would be a great loss to old Upper Upsalquitch if you were to leave." After a little more of that kind of stuff he shook my hand like he was afraid it hadn't been used lately and left.

On the way home it hit me: I'll bet that conniving old money grabber was the one that put Ned up to seeing me. I'll bet he intends to run for parliament himself—and wanted to be sure I wouldn't be in the way! Maybe I should change my mind just to spite him!

Monday March 24

Joe Azar came by today to go over the town books. He's a pretty conscientious treasurer. I didn't realize that the first quarter was coming to an end.

Everything seems to be in pretty good shape, though. Quite a few people are behind on their taxes but have always taken a "live and let live" attitude on this.

Annie just sends them monthly statements charging one per cent on the unpaid balance. So long as they keep those interest payments coming in to me, they know I won't report them to Joe.

Joe doesn't have to bother with details like that. We just look at the balance sheet together. After all, he doesn't have to worry about my personal affairs—at least so long as I don't do anything dishonest.

Tuesday March 25

Funny how fast you get attached to things. Had to go to the funeral for Annie's Uncle Casper this afternoon. And there, leading the procession, was Jim Dupuis driving *my* car! Gave me quite a turn. The black side curtains do dress it up a bit, though.

At graveside, I moved close to be sure the pallbearers didn't scratch it taking out the coffin.

Got it back tonight. Hope there's no rain. I've left it with the windows open. It certainly smells of flowers.

Wednesday March 26

Darned if Clare Latrouche didn't bring up her idea of a Town Income Tax again at Council tonight. I gambled and asked if the committee we had appointed was ready to report. As I had expected, they hadn't even had a meeting yet. So I played very stern and said I felt we needed action. Turning to Madame Latrouche, I asked her if she would take over as chairman. She jumped at the chance. Then I said we should feel out the public and asked Dan Prosser if he would take that on.

He's always had it in for Clare, so when I later explained what I had in mind, he could hardly wait to get started.

Beginning in the next issue of *The Portent* he will run a series of teaser ads like "What is TIT? Ask Councillor Latrouche" or "Is TIT the answer? Tell Councillor Latrouche how *you* would handle it."

Thursday March 27

Went to a movie tonight. With politics on my mind it seemed somehow suitable to see a re-run of "Gone With the Wind." Ned Dervish was there as usual, keeping a nervous eye on the till.

On a gamble I said to him in passing, "Sorry I had to give you a negative answer on Parliament, Ned. But I guess Casey is glad to know I won't be in his way."

Ned gave a kind of nervous laugh and kicked the popcorn machine, as if to make it work. But he didn't reply and I didn't press the point. There's no reason to offend him, seeing as how he's always been kind enough to shut his eyes whenever anyone uses my annual free pass.

Friday March 28

After writing up my diary last night I lay awake a long while just thinking about life. Wondering what it's all about. Used to have a friend who, when he got in his cups, would wander around asking "Why are we here?" Never heard him get a good answer.

Today, the mood is still on me. Annie says it's spring fever. Feels more like a fall chill to me. I suppose at my age, though, you've got to expect intimations of mortality.

It's getting harder and harder to put much zing into Browning's "Grow old along with me! The best is yet to be . . ." Some days the only thing that keeps me going is the thought that if I really put my mind to it I could sell old Casey an insurance policy.

Saturday March 29

The chill has passed. Woke up this morning full of zest and raring to take on the world. Then, recalling that it was Saturday morning, did the sensible thing. Rolled over and went back to sleep.

Was awakened about noon by the telephone. One of the farmers out on the Back Road, wanting to know if he could insure his mother-in-law against accidental death. Much as I hated to turn down business, I followed my instinct and told him I didn't carry mother-in-law insurance. (Of course it's not true. I'll insure a pig if they'll let it use the family name. But they're a bad lot out there on the Back Road and I had a hunch that maybe the accident had already happened.)

Palm Sunday
Sunday March 30

When I was a boy the church was always decorated on this day. Palms being a bit hard to find around here, we used willow branches and what flowers we could get. Now, they've abandoned the decorations for some reason. But the music is still the same—and I love it.

Didn't think the Reverend really got the most he could have out of the topic. To me, Christ's entry into Jerusalem-the-Golden, the crowds cheering and him riding quietly through them (probably having figured out what's ahead), is one of the most moving scenes in the Bible.

The poor guy! It's just like being Mayor when election time is coming up. Everybody is your friend until the curtain closes around them in the polling booth.

Monday March 31

Jim Dupuis came to get the car this morning and made some comment about keeping it clean. I admitted it was a little dusty. But I can't see how I can help him unless he accepts my suggestion: if he, as undertaker, wants the car kept clean then he, as Councillor, should arrange with the men in the Fire Department to keep his, the Fire Chief's vehicle washed. Maybe, as Mayor, I could manage to get a siren put on it for him. We don't get many fires but it sure would come in handy in parades.

April Fool's Day

Tuesday April 1

There should be a special day for Mayors. Out of 365 it seems reasonable to me that one should be set apart to honour not the man but the office. Perhaps if Upper Upsalquitch were to institute such a day other communities might follow.

If there's an April Fool's Day, why not a No Fool's Day?

A suitable celebration should, of course, include some sort of presentation; a gift to the Mayor from the hearts of the people. Like, maybe, government bonds.

I wonder who I can get to have this idea?

Wednesday April 2

Clare Latrouche arrived early for Council meeting tonight and after two minutes we knew the teaser campaign on Town Income Tax had really got to her. People had been coming up to her and saying all sorts of things like, "I suppose if we don't have TIT we'll go bust."

As soon as the meeting opened she resigned as committee chairman. Committeeman Bill Huggins asked, "Does that mean you're going to leave us flat?" Before she could say or do anything, I intervened to say that if the chairman wasn't prepared to support her own proposal, I felt the committee should be dissolved. No one objected and we moved on to more uplifting things.

Thursday April 3

Had an idea when I was shaving this morning. Thinking back to the way the car smelled of flowers after old Casper's last ride, I got to wondering about the waste there is in all those flowers that wilt in a day and are gone.

Called a fellow in Saint John who's an agent for artificial ones. He's going to send me down some sample wreathes and things.

Friday April 4

The first sign of Spring: had a magazine salesman at the door. Said he was working his way through college. I thought that one went out with the Charleston, unless he was taking a long course. Finally I decided, after he showed me a free atlas, that the Mayor should keep in touch with the world. Subscribed to his whole list. Always wanted an atlas. The Council may question what I'll get out of the women's magazines—but Annie won't.

Saturday April 5

Darned if Al Pines didn't run a story in *The Portent* on Clare Latrouche quitting her committee.

It was full of bad puns and in doubtful taste. I wish he had left well enough alone. But I guess being a small town editor gets to you after a while.

The heading, "TIT's Out For Clare Latrouche," was bad enough but he dragged in "a titillating concept" and suggested a slogan "TIT For Tax" and talked about "keeping abreast of the times."

I suppose she can't sue just because he said there was a visible cleavage in Council. But if I were Al, there's one subscription I wouldn't count on seeing renewed this year!

Easter Sunday

Sunday April 6

Saw people at church today I haven't seen for a year. Had trouble recognizing some of the women, though. The hats they wear these days!

The Reverend Angus was in fine style. Put it right on the line: he's not a rabbit lover. Down on coloured eggs, as well. I think he'd have gone on to putting down women for their Easter finery too, but his wife, Nellie, was sitting right under his nose in the front pew wearing a big purple hat topped with a yellow bird squatting on red and green daisies.

The choir was in its usual form, mis-handling "The Messiah."

The concept of resurrection has always appealed to me. I always make a point of paying off promptly on life insurance claims, but I'm religious enough to wait four days—just in case.

Monday April 7

Picked up an interesting tid-bit at Sim Jack's this morning: whatever his ambition at the federal level, Casey Irving would like to be the next mayor. (He'd probably be a good one.) Sort of wandered into the bank later to chat a spell. Told him what a shame it was that the Mayor got so little recognition. Led the conversation along to where he suggested maybe Upper Upsalquitch should have *one day a year* designated as Mayor's Day.

Told him it sounded like a great idea. Added that maybe the public should make a gift of, say, some government bonds, bought, of course, through the bank. He thought this was a sound suggestion.

I said I didn't think the idea should be put forward by a Councillor, so he's going to get his wife working on it.

Tuesday April 8

That siren I ordered for the car arrived today and Dan Prosser put it on for me. Called Jim Dupuis and asked him to meet me at the Fire Hall. Gave him time to get there first then drove up with the siren wailing for fair. It sure works! He was standing out front and I thought he'd lose his upper plate!

Now, the car is sort of *ex officio* part of the Fire Department, as well as being for the use of the Mayor and the funeral director.

Come to think of it, we're pretty progressive. I'll bet we're the only town in North America that has a hearse with a siren!

Wednesday April 9

The Council meeting looked pretty gay tonight. Had those samples of artificial wreathes and sprays from Saint John set up all around.

Set up a little presentation: as Fire Chief, Jim Dupuis told them how real flowers were a fire hazard; then Casey Irving talked about the sin of wasting money; next, I cued in Bill Huggins, as sort of our medical advisor, to talk about the effects of pollen on children.

That pretty well did it. By a unanimous vote we are the first town I know of to prohibit the use of fresh flowers at funerals and weddings.

Jim Dupuis gets to sell the artificial kind, I get ten per cent, and the car isn't going to smell any more.

Thursday April 10

Those people on the Back Road have been at it again. One of them got his hands on a detour sign and started diverting traffic off the Stewart Highway. Someone blocked the culvert where Grog Brook goes through and flooded the road. Then sat back with a team of horses and charged five dollars a car to pull people out.

As soon as I heard what was going on, I sent Milky Becker out to put a stop to it. Unfortunately, he got stuck in the mud himself and they let him sit there for four hours as their horrible example. They were able to get ten dollars a car after that.

It all ended abruptly, however, when one of the cars that showed up had a Mountie in it.

Friday April 11

Had a kind of annoying sequel this morning to yesterday's Back Road incident. When I had heard about Milky being up to his hub caps in mud, I admit I chuckled a bit. But I wasn't laughing this morning when I learned he had borrowed *my* car from Jim Dupuis. It took all morning for the Fire Department to get the muck off it. And I needed it for official business; I'm clean out of groceries.

Those Back Road people are going to hear about this! Mostly, we leave them alone and they sort of work things out for themselves. But when they start interfering with me, they'd better watch out.

Saturday April 12

This is the bad weekend. Each year, I make myself face up to doing my Income Tax, two weeks in advance of the deadline. That way, I figure, it gets in in time to avoid any penalties for late filing yet rides in on top of the rush and catches them when they haven't got time to worry about little details.

Got up at nine this morning and shaved and dressed just as if I were going out. Then pulled down all the blinds and spread out my papers.

It's at a time like this that you really feel lonely. Not a single dependent in the world! They took away my grandmother in Ireland five years ago. I sure miss her. We were so close that at times she seemed almost real.

Sunday April 13

After service this morning, asked the Reverend Angus if I could have a copy of his sermon. He was kind of flattered. Told him I wanted to send it to some people I knew in Ottawa. I figure that enclosing it with my tax forms can't do any harm. Especially if they read the title. Seems to me that "Judge Not That Ye Be Not Judged" is pretty damned pertinent.

I have a theory about government filing systems. Invoices, receipts, affidavits and so on they can handle. But there just can't be a place to put a tax return with a sermon attached. Even if they don't look at the theme of the sermon, figuring out what to do with it may take their minds off the contents.

Monday April 14

Man came to see me today. Wants to put us on a summer theatre circuit. He supplies the shows (cast, scenery, everything), we supply the place and help promote ticket sales. Says the whole town will profit.

After I mentioned my usual negotiation fee, he seemed to understand the problems of a mayor who has to work without a salary. It almost looked like a good thing for Upper Upsalquitch until I asked him about the plays.

He said they would be *Waiting For Godot* and *Lady Windermere's Fan*. I don't know about Lady Windermere but I was a Lady Chatterley fan when I was younger and I don't think we want *that* sort of thing going on in Upper Upsalquitch.

In a community like this you have to fight immorality every inch of the way. The alternatives are too costly.

Tuesday April 15

The theatre man called from Saint John. Said he had talked to his boss in Toronto but couldn't get me more than 10%. Lest he should feel that I am one of those people who knows the price of everything and the value of nothing, I told him that despite the narrow viewpoint of his boss, I would not stand in the way of culture, provided they changed the choice of plays.

He said the boss insisted on *Godot* but was willing to trade in *Lady Windermere's Fan* for *Who's Afraid of Virginia Woolf?* I said that sounded great; the kiddies would love it and would get the parents to attend. He sounded a little surprised. Guess he just hadn't thought of it that way.

Wednesday April 16

Told Council tonight about the summer theatre idea. They thought it was great. The question now is, where do we hold it? Named Clare Latrouche and Jim Dupuis as a committee to bring in a recommendation. I figure by the time they get through arguing, I'll have the problem solved.

Later, Ned Dervish, who loves his movie house, turned me down flat. Said if the plays come to town there will be folks coming here to see them, and he'll pick up more business that way than by cancelling his films and letting us use the stage.

Since it's the only stage big enough in town, I'm sure we'll get him to take the plays. What I don't know yet is how I'm going to persuade him.

Thursday April 17

Our national party in its infinitesimal wisdom has had the borders of our election district rearranged to include more people who are likely to vote for our team. In the process they have incorporated the village of Brunez and that means we get Ferdinand Leboeuf to represent us.

Ever since he was a cabinet minister, he's been dying to run again. Probably wants to re-capture his youth with the government typists. There's no way that Casey Irving (or anyone else) is going to win the nomination over him. Let Irving and Dervish and all see how they like *those* pommes!

Note: must get ahold of old Leboeuf and make sure he remembers me. If he's going to be our boy, the sooner he recalls that I was the one who got him off the hook ten years ago the better.

Friday April 18

Some people have been a little slow in taking out termite insurance. But I'm sure they'll come around. I do hope Dusty doesn't pressure them. All he has to do is make the point about having to burn the house down to prevent the termites from spreading and let it go at that.

Maybe I should have one house burned down as an example. There's a shack out on the Back Road that's been standing empty for years. No one knows who really owns it. By now it must be full of worm holes. I think Dusty should inspect it very carefully.

Saturday April 19

Got Dusty to go out to the Back Road first thing this morning (after I'd told him the problem). He came back pretty soon and said, "Sure looks like termites to me!"

Called Al Pines right away and told him what Dusty had discovered. Assured him that no house would be burned unless Council felt it necessary.

I'll give him a couple of issues to build the story up before I take it to Council. The insurance business should start perking up as soon as *The Portent* hits the streets.

Sunday April 20

Ah, day of rest and gladness
When we forget our badness
And shut our minds to madness!

Oh, Sunday is a glorious day!
At least, it sure would be that way,
If only I could make it pay!

Monday April 21

Had an idea while shaving this morning. About how to get the movie house for our summer theatre project. After nine, put through a call to the producer in Toronto and asked if they were planning to pick up any local talent for small parts. Told him our problem.

He said no. *Godot* requires just four actors and it's the same for the one about Virginia Woolf. I said, "Couldn't you write in a part? Seems to me four people is pretty slim fare. Why not slip in a teenage girl? It would add a little romance."

I didn't exactly catch what he said but it seemed negative. I told him Ned Dervish's daughter was pretty. (The truth is she's pretty awful. But I hear theatrical people can do wonders with makeup.) He perked up a mite at that and said next time he was down this way he would give her an audition. I hope it's a dark night.

Tuesday April 22

Told Mrs. Dervish that the theatrical people might want to audition her daughter. She seemed real interested. I'll let that soak for a couple of days.

Dusty Miller complained today that the boys at the Legion Hall don't treat the Termite Inspector with proper respect. Every time he drops in for a beer, someone calls out, "Hey fellows, here comes the town bugger!"

All I could offer him was sympathy. "Sometimes", I assured him, "the price of greatness is scorn."

Wednesday April 23

A delegation appeared before Council tonight. The Reverend Angus, Bill Ellis and Al Pines. They proposed that we have one day a year designated as Mayor's Day. Its purpose would be to foster an interest in civic government among the voters and school children. It was passed unanimously, Casey Irving having discreetly gone to the john, satisfied that his wife had prepared the delegation well.

Thursday April 24

Off tomorrow to the Maritime Mayors' Conference in Halifax. Decided to take Annie with me to make notes. At least, I think it was me that decided that. Lately, who decides what has been getting a little confused around this house.

Not that I mind very much. It's kind of nice so long as she doesn't go chasing me over to Clipper Hill's for a haircut too often or hiding my plus-fours again.

Annie is all excited about the trip. She has never been to a big city before. The idea that a place might have more than one bank in it is more than her upbringing can cope with.

When I mentioned to Council last night that I was going, her father gave me a strange kind of look. But whether he was registering parental concern or was worried for fear I was taking the town till with me I couldn't tell. If I had to bet, it would be on the money.

Friday April 25

Halifax. Might not be big by some folks' standards but it sure is big by ours. Big enough to have Annie jumping up and down like a kid. Soon as we got here she spotted all the stores and wanted to go shopping. I told her to take it easy or she'd use up our whole expense account. She said not to worry, we could save the taxpayers money in other ways.

Amazing. She never would have suggested anything as bold as that back home. What gets into women when they see a store? It's like an addiction. They'll say almost anything just to get inside.

Went to the opening meetings by myself. When I got back to the hotel had trouble rousing Annie on the phone. She was all walked out, not being used to those hard sidewalks, and had fallen asleep— surrounded by an array of dress boxes.

Finally got her up and going just in time to get to the annual dinner. Must say she looked real nice in her new things.

Saturday April 26

The meetings ended at noon today. Which is just as well since most of us were still hungover from the night before. After the dinner last night, someone suggested we should inspect the night life. Annie begged off to rest her feet. Just as well. Wouldn't have wanted a sweet, innocent girl like her exposed to the things we saw.

One place had two floor shows. The first was pretty decent, but the second (in the basement) certainly wasn't worth the five dollars extra we each had to pay. In fact, it was pretty disgusting. After a couple of hours we all walked out.

Sunday April 27

Got back home late last night. Tried to pull together some notes on what had happened at the meetings. Unfortunately, the only firm suggestion I remember making was to adjourn.

One good thing does come out of these sessions, though: you realize you're not alone in your misery.

When I read my paper on "The Mayor's Abuse Level," I'm not sure they understood me too well. (It was Saturday morning.) But there were cries of, "You can say that again!" etc. And old Jim McDonald from West Inverness just sat there after I was through, shaking his head and muttering "The bastards." I could see he was really moved.

Monday April 28

Met Ned Dervish's daughter on the street today. The minute I saw her I knew her mother had told her about the audition. She'd bleached her hair and taken to wearing false eyelashes. And there were a couple of lumps in her sweater that I swear weren't there the last time I saw her. She looks like a tart smuggling grapefruit.

She stopped to chat but was so busy fanning her eyes and juggling her fruit, I'm not sure she heard me when I told her maybe the theatre people wouldn't be coming after all because we hadn't been able to find them a proper place to put on their plays. Anyhow, we'll see if her ears are real.

Tuesday April 29

Yep, they're real! Ned Dervish was around to see me first thing this morning. Said he'd been thinking a lot about the summer theatre project and had come to realize it would be a good thing for Upper Upsalquitch. As a citizen, he felt he should make a contribution and so, if we hadn't already made any firm commitment, he was prepared to offer the movie house.

I said I thought we could probably arrange to accept his offer.

Wednesday April 30

Council was delighted to know that Ned had changed his mind. Clare Latrouche and Jim Dupuis looked mighty relieved. Now they can get back to not speaking to each other.

After the meeting got Al Pines aside and made a little deal on printing the tickets. I didn't want to be too direct so I persuaded him to run lots and then turn them over to me for safekeeping.

I figure I can get the Girl Guides working and we'll split the take on a special charity night. That plus the 10% the producer promised me should make it all worthwhile.

Thursday May 1

Ever since I rammed through the by-law that keeps Casey Irving from throwing his delinquent tenants out before warm weather, May 1st has been called "Moving Day" around here.

On April 30th, Casey can turn off the heat and start evicting. Trouble is, for every non-paying tenant he throws out, another moves in. He's a very patient man. He gets them all to sign notes at his bank for what they owe. When he adds all the notes together as assets, the bank looks like Big Business!

I don't understand these things but I have a hunch that any man who keeps his cash in a toilet has already figured a way for *this* to work for him, too.

All of which reminds me of one of those facts I have in my head that isn't of much use. *The Farmer's Almanac* says that the Anglo Saxons used to call this month *Thrimilce* because the cows could be milked three times daily. Going from Casey to that is probably what you call free association, although "free" is not a word that tends to come to mind when you think of Casey.

Friday May 2

One must always show proper concern for others. It's the test of a gentleman and a must for mayors.

That's why I went to see old Seward in the hospital today. Sat with him quite a while. A sad case. To be that old and that rich and have no one to leave your money to!

I must go back often. It would be good for his health if he could come to feel that I'm the son he never had.

Saturday May 3

Had a very flattering letter yesterday from Rory "Big Dan" McLeod, the mayor of East Baddeck. He said my paper at the Mayors' Conference had been of real personal help to him. Confessed that he had always been very sensitive to all the abuse a mayor gets—without ever realizing it comes with the job. Now, having heard my talk and having started to apply my formula, he says he's getting quite MAL-adjusted.

Not being the sort of man who can leave someone else's pun alone, wrote him back today and said I hoped he would find my paper a malaprop if he ever had to share a den with the rivals.

Sunday May 4

Going through some things in the cupboard this afternoon while looking for a stamp I had peeled off a return envelope one time, I came on a picture of Grandpa Heber. Taken, I would guess, about ten years before he died in his home in Boston.

Fine looking man. It was sad the way he went downhill in his later years. Made a lot of money when he was younger. Discovered a use for used crankcase oil: spill some on a corner of the family farm, sell the land to speculators, and move to the city. Fast.

From that he went into real estate in earnest. Probably half the stories I used to hear about him when I was a kid were made up by his in-laws. I can't really believe that he actually persuaded someone to buy property for retirement on Revere Beach by claiming it was a religious community. Or that he got a couple in the Midwest to invest in shares of Boston Common.

Rich and lonely in his final years, he went a little wonky. Ended up leaving his wealth to a foundation for buying deodorant for Zulus or something. Which is why his picture was in the cupboard. I don't like to be reminded of how close I once came to inheriting all that money.

Monday May 5

A government man came to see me today. Said he was a pollution expert. Told him we didn't need an expert; we were doing pretty well on our own.

No sense of humour. Wants to hold a Town Meeting and show a film. Guess there's no harm in that. Called the Reverend Angus and asked for the use of the church for Friday night. He said it would mean cancelling choir practice. I told him not to worry; the congregation would never notice.

He replied, and rather sharply, "Instead of criticizing the choir all the time, why don't you do something to help improve it?" Good point. Promised him I'd give it some thought.

But I really haven't the faintest idea of how to go about improving the choir, unless we could hide a metronome in the baptismal font.

Tuesday May 6

Saw old Seward again today. He seems to be failing rapidly. But I think he's still of pretty sound mind.

Told him of my dreams to make Upper Upsalquitch a better place to live in. Talked about the needs of our children, especially the orphans.

There were tears in old Seward's eyes when I got through. I felt a little moist myself. If only I had the money to help!

Wednesday May 7

Al Pines having run two good feature stories on the termite-infested shack on the Back Road, I took copies of the stories to Council tonight and, having read them aloud, suggested that it was up to us to do something about it. Right away Casey Irving—who I know has always had trouble collecting his rents out that way— said, "I think we should burn the place down before the termites spread!" (meaning to the other places he owns).

Everyone agreed and the motion was passed unanimously. They wanted to have the Fire Department go to it tomorrow but I suggested in the interest of safety that we wait until next week to give the Fire Chief a chance to survey the scene.

Thursday May 8

Casey Irving told me today he had had a call from old Seward's lawyer. Apparently, the old boy is changing his will!

Friday May 9

Had a letter from Cousin Ralph today. He does the hiring for his firm. An Equal Rights group descended on him last week because he had refused to hire a black girl. Then another group came in because he had refused to hire a Frenchman for the same job.

Said he brought them together in his boardroom, served them coffee and left them alone for half an hour. They filed out pretty silent.

Meantime, he hired a Swedish girl "for personal reasons." He hopes there's no protest pending from Women's Lib or the Gay Liberation Front.

Saturday May 10

Man out on the Back Road called this morning to ask if there was such a thing as animal insurance. Told him it wasn't very common but if he had the money for premiums I felt sure we could work something out. Asked him what kind of animals he wanted to insure. He hedged a bit and wanted to know if he couldn't just insure what he owned without going into details. I just laughed and hung up.

That's the Back Road for you! He'd think nothing of sticking me for the insurance—and not have the courtesy to invite me to their Saturday night cock fights!

Sunday May 11

Spent a pleasant and profitable Sunday afternoon. Drove over to Brunez and paid a social call on Ferdinand Leboeuf. He welcomed me most warmly. I apologized for arriving un-announced but he assured me he was only reading. (Which, I guess, was true. I could see the corner of a *Playboy* sticking out of the family Bible.)

Told him I had heard he was planning to run again. He admitted that he might have to give in to popular demand if it seemed in the best interests of the country.

I pointed out now that Upper Upsalquitch was in his riding there were a lot of voters who had never been exposed to him before. While he was mulling that over, I said he could be sure I would support him to the hilt "as I did once before in another sense." That made him blink. It was rough to have to remind him that ten years ago a particular chicken of his had come home to roost.

He got the message. If I help him get elected I'll have me a member of parliament that might be very attentive to my needs.

Monday May 12

Had a little fun this morning. I was walking by as Casey was unlocking the bank door. Stopped to chat and went in with him. Suddenly, I said, "Excuse me," and headed toward the john at the back. He came bounding after me like a hungry spaniel. But I beat him to the door and got in first.

On lifting the lid in standard male fashion, I saw it. Sure enough! There in a plastic bag was the wealth of Upper Upsalquitch!

Casey was very flustered. But I assured him that the Mayor was the last person who would talk, especially since a few of those dollars belong to me.

Tuesday May 13

The termite insurance is beginning to sell. It was a little slow at first. But then I increased Dusty's commission and things began to happen. I don't know what he's telling them, but I do know one thing: it's not hard to sell insurance when the prospective buyer calls you up in a panic.

Wednesday May 14

My experience at the bank on Monday led me to propose to Council that we should have a town safe.

Dan Prosser, who has a dirty mind, said something about that really being a problem for the Public Health Committee. But I pounded my gavel so the rest couldn't hear him and pointed out that we had no protection for our records.

After a bit of steering I got what I wanted: we'll just buy the bank's safe and have it repaired. I got enough money approved, so that Casey can afford the new safe I've ordered for him.

Casey was so pleased that he didn't ask his annual question about the cost of the Mayors' Conference trip. *Quid pro quo*—and just as well, seeing how much of the money went on his daughter's back.

Thursday May 15

Biggest fire in the history of Upper Upsalquitch! Half the town turned out to see the Fire Department burn down the termite-infested shack. I chose to stay away. When folks asked me why I wasn't going I muttered something about being afraid that termites, like fleas, might be germ carriers. I doubt if my comment did much good, but every little bit helps.

Apparently, everything went off pretty well although the Fire Department may have been a little embarrassed. They had decided to have their pumper there, just in case. As the fire died down, they turned on the pumper to drown the ashes but they had it hooked up backwards. Instead of shooting out water, they just blew bubbles in Grog Brook. I hope Al Pines didn't get a picture of *that!*

Friday May 16

Milky Becker came in to see me this afternoon, looking a mite uncomfortable. Says he went out to the Back Road last night because he had gotten a tip that there was going to be a cock fight. But when he tried to arrest the first man that showed up he was told to come and see me. "You can't touch me," says the man, "I've got insurance."

The very idea! To talk like that to an officer of the law! And before even a cent of money has changed hands! There's so much dishonesty in the world today you wonder how humanity survives! And now if I do sell those people insurance on their birds, Milky will expect a cut.

Saturday May 17

Well, I'll say this for the Back Roadents, they're not all bad. This morning the guy who told Milky he was insured showed up to apologize. I was inclined to be pretty stern, but decided when he pulled out a fat wallet it was better to forgive and receive.

I quoted him what I felt was a fair rate. To my surprise, he not only paid but asked if I would insure ten of his friends. When I said it would only be fair to extend the same privilege to everyone, he banged down enough money for the lot and produced a list of their names.

Got ahold of Milky this afternoon and gave him a little talk on the importance of developing local sports. Gave him two dollars a head to see that the boys on the Back Road had proper protection from the unwholesome influence of people coming to town with larger roosters.

Sunday May 18

What a strange lot women are! It was pouring rain and blowing hard last night when Annie got up to go home. I persuaded her to stay over and use the spare room. Heard her up and stirring early. This is the one morning of the week I have always relished being by myself. I just didn't think ahead last night. But there she was, so—to make the best of it—I asked her to stay a while longer and make breakfast. She finally agreed. But darned if, first, she didn't slip out the back door, come around to the front and knock until I could get there to let her in. Said it was important to keep up appearances. I didn't have the nerve to point out that any neighbour that could see her at the front door could also have seen her coming around from the back.

If she was worried about appearances, she should have realized she gave the appearance of being nuts. But it *was* a good breakfast.

Later, when I saw her in church and nodded she actually had the courage to smile back.

Victoria Day

Monday May 19

A Victorious Day! Today the fur vest I ordered through Eaton's catalogue last November arrived. Just in time for tulip picking. Took four letters, including one to Mr. Timothy Eaton himself (returned marked "No Forwarding Address") before I was able to make myself understood.

Just couldn't get across the fact that although I entered my dimensions in the wrong column on the order form, that did *not* necessarily make me a woman. They kept suggesting politely that I should re-check my measurements, that perhaps I had them in the wrong order.

Finally got the vest though. All it took in the end was a note saying: "Please send as ordered. I have a low bust."

Tuesday May 20

More mail and this time a new set of rates from Perpetual Life. Everything is getting more expensive these days. It gets harder and harder to make your dollars stretch.

Fortunately, on checking the rates I found I've been charging well over their prices anyway. Felt tremendously relieved. It's nice to know that I've been protecting my customers against increases all along.

Wednesday May 21

For some time have been enjoying the way Annie prepares fiddleheads, those little fern shoots that grow down along Grog Brook. Cooks them like spinach. Just great!

Got to thinking, it's a shame not to share this delicacy with the rest of the world. Nova Scotia has its dulse, Boston has its beans. Upper Upsalquitch could become the home of the fiddlehead.

At Council meeting tonight suggested that we should try to get someone to set up a fiddlehead factory.

Mixed reaction. Always that way when I propose bringing in a little industry. They understand that it could mean lower taxes but at heart they like our town the way it is—untainted by progress.

Thursday May 22

Ever since that government man held the Town Meeting on pollution there have been rumblings. Seems foolish to me. Our water must be healthy or there wouldn't be so many weeds growing in it.

However, one must bend with the times so I've gotten an option on Pres Philhower's old farm on the Back Road. The town may have to buy some property for a sewage plant. But before anything is bought or sold, there are a few questions that I, as Mayor, feel I must ask. Like, is there a market for processed sewage? If it's good as fertilizer, then I'd better get a fertilizer man on the line and make a deal. If not, what will it cost to put in sewers? And who do I know who will give us a good price? Since this is a one-time job, I think 10% is too little.

Friday May 23

The Mayor is a leader and must retain control, no matter what the cost.

Pondering the sewer problem, I don't mind 10% on road work because it goes on forever. But it wouldn't be fair to my rank to take only 10% on a one-time deal. Mayors have to have standards and stick to them. If you don't, you lose respect.

Saturday May 24

Told Annie my idea about a fiddlehead factory and had her do a little research. She reports that getting one going may be a bit of a problem. Seems she and I have been eating, personally, about 50% of the local crop. That doesn't leave much to share with the rest of the world.

In addition, there are already people who package fiddleheads somewhere else around here. That shows that at least I had a good idea. Just got hung up on the First Law of Supply and Demand: don't worry about the demand if you haven't got any supply.

Sunday May 25

Got something out of the sermon for a change today. The Reverend Angus was hanging his hat on Solomon's Ecclesiastes. Quoted from it: "Cast thy bread upon the waters: for thou shalt find it after many days."

This never made sense to me before. Couldn't see the merit in getting back a lot of soggy bread. Realized today that probably what the old boy was writing about was what we call around here "chumming."

Every guide does it when his American tourist isn't looking. Throws out a handful of bread to attract the fish. Only difference here is you don't have to wait many days to get it back. It shows up right away in tips.

Monday May 26

Telephone repairman came today. I've been having trouble with static on the line. Should have a private phone but it's expensive. And listening in on the other parties is a good way of keeping in touch with what's going on. (Trying to control the tide of public opinion by having a finger on the Watergate, you might say.)

Tuesday May 27

Old Seward passed away today. A grand old man. Too few appreciated him properly. People said he was a skin-flint but I know better. He was just shy. Wonder when the new will is supposed to be read?

Wednesday May 28

Had an idea while shaving this morning. Saw a government bulletin the other day, offering to help farmers who want to plant rape seed. Not sure whether rape will grow here, nor quite what you do with it if it does. But if the government has some money to put into it, there's no harm in trying.

Asked the councillors for permission to write for more information. Joe Azar said, "I don't know if we should encourage such a thing. Enough people around here are getting away with murder!"

Thursday May 29

Finally found the best contractor for the sewer job. Bill McDonald, a boyhood friend, says he'll bid and I've got two other quotes lined up just in case. Come next Council, we'll open the bids.

Bill's price looks like the best—but not by much. I sure hope he knows what a sewer looks like!

Friday May 30

Was called down to Casey's office this morning. Old Seward's lawyer was in town and wanted to discuss the will. Put on my best suit. I should have gone in plus-fours. He left all his money to a young nurse in the hospital—and sent me his regrets. *Sic transit.*

Went home and spent the afternoon in front of the TV set. Big event of the day down in the U.S. of A. was the Indianapolis 500, a pretty exciting car race. Kind of intrigued by the reaction of the crowds along the track. For people taking a day off to commemorate the tragedy of those who died for peace, they sure sounded awful violent and forgetful.

Saturday May 31

Annie stopped by for a while this afternoon. Did a washing for me. Then asked me to do her a favour: please stop talking about fiddle-heads.

Had to admit that when I get an idea I hate to let go. Also admitted that all the pots with green water she found in the kitchen this morning were from secret late-night experiments.

We cleaned them up together and that will be the end of it. Once I get the stains out of the sink.

Sunday June 1

After church I rolled up my sleeves and went at it. A couple of hours later the sink was its old self again.

It was kind of sad, pouring those good gallons of fiddlehead consommé down the drain. But I have to be honest with myself: if someone had served it to me at a dinner I would have wondered what it was. Without meaning to, I think what I really invented was a swamp.

Monday June 2

Today the library caught fire. Before the Volunteer Fire Brigade could get on the wagon, both books were destroyed. And one of them hadn't even been coloured in yet.

Mustn't be bitter like that: We could have more books if the voters really wanted them. But our kind of people spend so much time gossiping that, even before they start to read, their lips are already tired.

Tuesday June 3

That fire at the library yesterday did *some* good: next time, the boys in the Fire Brigade will remember that you always have to fasten the hose to the pumper. Jim Dupuis looked awful silly standing there yelling "Pump harder!" with the end of the hose lying on the street behind him.

He said afterward that he *knew* it wasn't connected. "If it had been," he explained, "I wouldn't have been able to get the nozzle close to the flames."

You can't beat Jim for knowing his own weaknesses.

Wednesday June 4

Special Council meeting tonight to decide what to do about the library. Bill Huggins said he didn't mind still having it in his drugstore but it *had* been crowding the toothpaste display a bit. If we didn't mind he would like to put it back to where it used to be, by the suppositories.

We voted on that and it was passed with Madame Latrouche abstaining in a very ladylike way. We then voted money for a new shelf. When the question of what books to buy came up, I adjourned the meeting so the councillors could think up the names of a few on their own. Dan Prosser said we should write to the Carnegie Foundation for suggestions but I didn't want to open *that* can of worms.

Thursday June 5

The Girl Guides are doing pretty well on the ticket sales for charity night at the summer theatre. I sure hope it rains that night! I figure as of now they've sold about two and a half tickets for every seat in the house. But I haven't the heart to discourage them. They're so full of enthusiasm! I must say it does my heart good to see them trudging door to door and collecting two dollars a head.

Friday June 6

Mayor's Day. Everything went well. I was a little disappointed in the size of the gift, but considering the school kids had only been saving for a month, it wasn't bad.

As I pointed out to Casey the Ambitious, this is only the first year. It will probably grow. Next year, perhaps we can get the shop-keepers to match the kids dollar for dollar. A little more competition among grades might be a good thing. His wife should also get Clare Latrouche to speak to Father Ignatius about holding a bingo the night before. He understands the relationship between Church and State pretty well. After all, he's the only priest I know whose house-keeper is collecting the Family Allowance. In fact, she's probably claiming the entire Holy Family.

Saturday June 7

Was I glad to see this afternoon end! As Mayor, I had to open the annual Upper Upsalquitch Flower Show. When I stood up to make the required speech I suddenly realized that I couldn't remember from last year what it's all in aid of. Still can't. But I hedged—which was probably a suitable thing to do on such an occasion—and commended the ladies for their efforts "on behalf of so worthy a cause."

The real horror was then having to go up and down the rows of trestle tables admiring the plants.

I'm a duffer at knowing the names of plants. If a stranger asks me what some local flower is, I always say, "Well, I don't know what you call it in your part of the world, but here I've always heard it referred to as Grandfather's Beard!"

Sunday June 8

We have a nice little custom in our church, carried over from when it was Methodist. The second Sunday in June is called Children's Day. The children used to bring flowers and pile them around the communion table. Now, each brings a little gift for a shut-in. The flowers were nice but this is more practical and, I think, significant.

As I sat there watching them march up the aisle, must admit I had a twinge of regret for never having had any children of my own. What, with them playing in my bushes and writing dirty words on my walk on Hallowe'en, it's not a twinge I get very often.

But when you see them all cleaned up and quiet in church, you forget what hellcats they are when left on their own. Who knows, maybe if I hadn't had to look after Mother in her last, long years I might have found some girl, married her, and begat.

Well, it's too late now! Who would want a father who wears plus-fours and coughs his way to the breakfast table? Of course, I *could* adopt. Lord knows, the morals of this community are such as to make the supply no problem!

Monday June 9

Annie has been after me to take a holiday. Says it would do me good to get away. My political instincts tell me that a reasonable translation of what she is saying would be "We had a good time in Halifax. Let's do it again."

It's really not a bad idea. I did enjoy being in Halifax and having her with me. The trouble is I have a moral block: it has never seemed right to me to spend money travelling at my own expense. I suppose there are people who do it, but that doesn't excuse the rest of us. Maybe I'll write to my cousin Ralph to see if he knows of any meetings that a mayor should attend.

Tuesday June 10

The disappointment from old Seward's oversight has subsided somewhat. Been talking to the young nurse he left all his money to. Charming girl. Annie's away visiting her aunt so I invited the nurse over for tea.

Finally got around to discussing the money. Seems she hasn't decided what to do with it. I suggested that since old Seward had expressed a desire to do something for others, it might be a fine thing—as well as a good investment—if she were to lend the money to the town so we could build a new hospital.

For some reason she seemed a little hesitant. But when I mentioned it would have a special section of private rooms for older men and she would be in charge of that whole section, she became quite interested.

Wednesday June 11

Darn Annie! I finally got that note written to cousin Ralph, then found that Annie had taken the key to the petty cash box with her. Result, no stamp. Had to go down to the drugstore and *buy* one. Sure hope I remember to collect from her when she comes back.

Eight cents may not seem much to some people, but eight cents a day is $29.20 a year—almost 3% on a thousand dollars. If I kept this up I'd be licked.

Thursday June 12

Annie's still away, so invited the young nurse back for tea again. She came. Never met so forthright a young lady. Wastes little time on amenities.

She's made up her mind; she'll lend the money. What a wonderful thing for Upper Upsalquitch! I think I can get a matching grant from the government, and we'll have a hospital we can all be proud of! It looks as though that lot I own is finally going to get sold.

Friday June 13

Friday the 13th! And the only one this year. It's a good thing I'm not superstitious. A lot of people are. And they waste a great deal of time over it, too. But I just go my way, and so far nothing has ever happened. (Touch wood.)

Father Ignatius once told me he dreads Friday the 13th. Many of his parishioners are bothered more by it than Good Friday. They get in the confessional and won't shut up. He said he has thought of having a tape recording made that just says, over and over again, "Is that a fact!"—so he can get free once in a while to go to the can.

Saturday June 14

After delaying it as long as I could in the hope Annie would take pity on me, got down to doing a little tidying up around the house today. Annie keeps the office in great shape and she always cleans up in the kitchen, but she doesn't seem to take much interest in the rest of the house—except the area in front of the TV set. I know I'm pressing my luck, but I *have* hinted a couple of times that the place is getting kind of dusty.

When I was through running the dust mop around, I leaned it against the TV set, put a bottle of furniture polish and a rag beside it. Then I got out that hot water bottle Dan Prosser gave me, filled it and put it in my chair.

Unfortunately, she didn't come by tonight so I'll have to leave the props there until Monday. Looks a little messy if anyone drops in but I'll have to take my chances. Maybe there'll be a cobweb on the mop handle by the time she gets here, if I can find a nice big spider.

Sunday June 15

I realize now that part of what I felt in church last week was self pity. This is Father's Day and the twinge came back as I looked at all the children scrubbed and shining with their gift-tie-wearing fathers.

Well, there's no room in life for self pity. It's a luxury I can't afford. Nor is there any profit in thinking what might have been. There *was* a girl once, and I was ready to marry her any time she'd have me. But when I told her, she only laughed and said thirteen was too young. She was sixteen then. When I became sixteen I still loved her. But then she was nineteen and went away to college and never came back.

Now I find my mind turning more and more to marriage. Marriage with Annie? Would it work? I'm pulled in two directions: I don't want to rush into anything until I'm sure—yet, if I don't hurry up, there won't be much time left.

When you're young you think you have all the time there is. And when you get older you realize just how *little* that is. If I don't decide soon I may go up the aisle with "Time's winged chariot" right on my heels.

Monday June 16

Who do I know in construction that has some real building experience? Ten percent on a hundred thousand isn't that hard to understand, even if you've never seen a blueprint. If only old Seward could see the good his money is going to do!

Annie has just returned and heard all about our plans. She reminded me that the hospital will need to be properly equipped. She's right. I wonder who else is getting old—and has money? Must speak to my young nurse about that!

Remembered to collect that money from Annie for the stamp. Arranged for her to leave the key in the toothbrush mug from now on.

Tuesday June 17

Saw Father Ignatius today. Asked him if last Friday was as bad as other Fridays that fell on the 13th. "Worse," he said. "There was a line-up of people waiting to confess. I slipped away to the men's room at one point. No sooner got seated in a cubicle than a man entered the next one, sat down, and said "Father, I have sinned. . . .""

Wednesday June 18

Council very enthusiastic tonight about hospital plans. Casey is handling the bond issue for the nurse. Government grant approved by phone. The architect has sent over the blueprints I bought from him. (Actually, it's one of the draftsmen that is selling them, having clipped off the name of the hospital they were originally used for.)

Bill Dogood is going to build it. Hope he'll be able to handle the project. Closest thing he's done to hospitals is making a road bed. But, as he says, "There has to be a first time for everything!"

Thursday June 19

Letter from Cousin Ralph today about possible meetings for mayors. He's found an excellent one: a conference in mid-July on pollution in the Great Lakes. With all that concern the government man stirred up with his Town Meeting, I feel that I owe it to the voters to keep abreast of the latest developments.

Friday June 20

With more warning than you'd expect, a national election has been called for September 17th. Monsieur Leboeuf knows I can deliver the vote in Upper Upsalquitch and is being very nice to me—just as nice as *I* will be to *him* when we get him elected and he can deliver some business out of Ottawa.

People who think politics is dishonest just don't understand. It's really the most honest business there is. It operates wholly by the Golden Rule—although sometimes we're shy to admit it. That's why we sometimes paraphrase the Rule into saying, "You scratch my back and I'll scratch yours." But the spirit is still the same.

Saturday June 21

At Annie's suggestion I wrote another letter to Cousin Ralph. After thanking him for discovering that convention of polluters, asked his advice on where to stay. They say big city hotel prices are something terrible.

I don't know, but if Annie suggests again that we cut costs by booking just one room, maybe I'll weaken. We're getting pretty close together now. I haven't had the courage to put my arm around her or kiss her yet and she still calls me "Mayor," but there's something in the air between us that's warm and personal. Being near her is like standing in front of an open fire on a cold winter day. Just hope I don't get burned.

Sunday June 22

Well, that's over! The annual dinner with the Reverend Angus and his wife, Nellie. I appreciate that he feels he has to make the gesture (and I feel I have to accept). But since we both are impelled by a sense of obligation, it puts a strain on the occasion from the start.

Luckily, Nellie is a good cook—which eases the strain on the inner man. And she has a fine figure. As the Reverend Angus carved up the roast and the Catholics, I found myself engaging in some pleasant speculation about Nellie's non-culinary abilities.

However, one can prolong such pleasantness only so long. After dinner, coffee in the living-room found us deep in the problems of the world. Since I could see little hope that the Reverend and I were going to solve them, I took my leave as soon as seemed proper. Now, we can both relax for another year.

Monday June 23

A travelling photographer stopped in today and offered to take my picture free. I'm not inclined toward that sort of thing. But he was a nice young man—and the price was right. He explained that if he could show people he had taken me, it would help sell them. I was tempted to argue the logic but figured it was his business.

Annie was upset because I wouldn't go to the barber first. Told her *that* was silly. I am what I am, no matter what the length of my hair. And if I spend money letting Clipper Hill go at my head, then it wouldn't be a free photo.

I did put on a clean shirt and tie though, as a concession. To please Annie, I chose the tie she gave me for Christmas. Of course this will mean she'll have an extra shirt to wash and iron this week, but she didn't seem to mind. After all, it's part of her job.

Tuesday June 24

Had a meeting today with Melba Springer, the head of the Girl Guides. We've been saying the theatre tickets they've been selling were for charity, but so far no one has announced *what* charity. I like things buttoned down. She agreed the girls should choose something specific.

I brought up the theme of "Good Citizenship" and pointed out that the girls should do something for the community as a whole. When she pressed me for an idea I pointed out that Upper Upsalquitch has a Mayor but the Mayor doesn't really have a proper office. I said I would be glad to continue contributing my front parlour if the Guides wanted to decorate it. She thinks it's a great idea and has gone off to discuss it with them. Boy, I thought I'd *never* get that room papered!

Wednesday June 25

Man named Girlen (I think that's what he said) telephoned me long
distance today for an appointment. Wouldn't say much about why he
wanted to see me except that it was "in our mutual interest." That
phrase always bothers me. It usually means, that what is mutual is
something *I've* got that the other fellow wants to get free.

But I've agreed to see him on Friday, so we'll soon know.

Council meeting was very dull tonight. Barely a quorum. All sorts
of excuses sent along. Truth is, we're having a hot spell and nobody
that doesn't have to is going to get up off his porch and shut himself
in a small room with a lot of other heavy sweaters.

Thursday June 26

My file of foreign mail is growing. Two letters today. One from the
the Great Lakes–Ontario Probe (GLOP) saying I'd be most welcome
to attend their July 10th and 11th meetings as an observer. (It costs a
lot just to look: they enclosed a Registration Fee invoice for $50.00.)

The other letter was from Cousin Ralph, suggesting a couple of
hotels. He had been kind enough to enclose leaflets from them.

Annie got replies off confirming our attendance and asking for
reservations at the nicest-sounding hotel. I was afraid for a while she
was going to get into the "one room or two?" topic again, but I guess
she lost her nerve. Just as well; I wouldn't want anything like that
in our files while we were away.

Friday June 27

Mr. Girlen showed up today, as agreed. Arrived from Fredericton Airport in a rented car with a rented driver. Apparently accustomed to doing things in a big way. Came bouncing into the house like he was bringing me First Prize in the Irish Sweepstakes. Damn near shook my hand off.

Seems he has wonderful news for all the residents of Upper Upsalquitch. Recent research indicates we may be sitting on top of very rich uranium deposits! (I don't know how they get to know these things without ever having been here, but who am I to argue with people that can afford rented cars and drivers?)

Mr. Girlen wants my support in getting the residents to agree to a survey. After a fair bit of chat, I agreed to let him have a decision next week. He had another try at getting my hand off, and left.

Saturday June 28

Spent a good part of today thinking about Mr. Girlen. He has a fancy title—but *I* mark him down as a stock promoter. When he was talking about that survey and what would be involved, it came out that he was forming a special company just to handle this wonderful opportunity. He conceded he might just possibly be willing to let us local folks buy some of the stock in it—even before the survey. (He admitted that if the survey didn't turn up anything, afterwards might be a poor time to buy.) In return for my cooperation, he has offered me a block of stock free.

While I love getting something for nothing, if that survey draws a blank it will be getting nothing for nothing—and a lot of my voters will have been hurt. It's a tough decision to make.

Sunday June 29

After my customary pleasant start on a Sunday morning, got up and prepared to go to church. However, Annie called and asked if I'd like to go for a picnic. It was a beautiful day and the prospect of sitting in a hot church didn't seem too appealing. She made up a lunch and with it braced between the rollers in the back of the car, we took off for the open spaces.

Found a nice quiet spot on the bank of the river up past the rapids and well away from where the voters wander. Spread a black quilt that Jim Dupuis keeps in the car. Took off my shirt and got a bit of a burn.

What a wonderfully relaxing experience! We should do this more often. It's so important for people to get out and enjoy the sun that I spent part of the time trying to figure out some kind of weather insurance I could offer.

Monday June 30

Broke ground today for the hospital. Good crowd. Made a short speech: "It's more generous to give than to receive." Didn't see anyone in the crowd reach for his wallet, though.

I've got the bed deal sewn up, but haven't found a contact yet in linen and blankets. Well, you can't win them all. The electrician has been very cooperative. He's going to re-wire the house while he's at it.

Dominion Day

Tuesday July 1

Dominion Day, the official birthday of Canada. And, this year, the occasion of the best Mayor's Picnic ever.

Of course, we had the usual little problems. Joe Azar's annual trick of serving a hot dog bun with his finger in it made Letty Hinch throw up. But then she's thrown up at every picnic for the last forty years. (Whatever happened to the girl who just *swooned*?)

Sim Jack closed his laundry for the day because we needed all the laundry bags for the sack race. Being a gentleman, he decided to enter himself lest he be accused of just creating work for himself.

Both the race and his egg rolls were a great success.

Wednesday July 2

The big topic at Council meeting tonight was last night's fireworks display. There was some heavy joking about how the event went off. But the truth is we all had a pretty bad scare.

No one is quite sure what happened. My suspicion is that Dusty Miller flicked a lit cigar butt into the bag. In any case, it was all over very quickly. Sky rockets, roman candles, pinwheels—the whole glorious mix—went off with a whoosh and a roar. And everyone headed for cover.

Sim Jack, who is always the man in charge (at this time of the year the other councillors call him "Cracker Jack"), took off too. He was sitting right beside the bag when she went. He shot straight up in the air and was running before his feet touched the ground.

The kids all thought it was great while it lasted. Trouble is they wanted us to do it again.

Next year we'll have to be more careful. And *I* will have to make it my personal business to keep Dusty Miller at a safe distance.

Thursday July 3

Called Mr. Girlen today. (He had asked me to call him collect. It had never occurred to me that people place long distance calls any other way!)

Told him he could go ahead with the survey but only on one condition: he would have to see that that block of stock he offered me was sold before the survey results came out. He argued a bit. Said I might be passing up a chance to be a millionaire. I said it was better not to be a shareholder if things went bad, and if I had to choose on what seemed like fifty-fifty odds between being a millionaire and being lynched, I'd be willing to pass up wealth for health. He finally agreed.

As soon as he has the company set up (I suspect that means as soon as the shares are printed), he'll let me know and I'll break the good news to the people.

Independence Day

Friday July 4

Tonight was the opening of our summer theatre. It being the start of the long Independence Day weekend for our American friends, we had a fair sprinkling of summer visitors and tourists in the audience.

It was a packed house. In fact, it was a little too packed. I guess the Girl Guides and I did get sort of carried away on selling those charity tickets.

However, after the first ten minutes of "Waiting For Godot" there were plenty of seats for everyone. As Mayor, I had to stick it out. It's the price you have to pay.

I have to be honest with myself. I checked out all the aspects of this project except one: I forgot to ask if the company could act. This is obviously too tough a play for a road company to handle. Even a capable road company. Perhaps what appealed to them was the fact that they didn't have to spend much on scenery.

Tomorrow night they'll present "Who's Afraid of Virginia Woolf?" Already, I know the answer: I am.

Saturday July 5

Took my courage in hand and went back to the movie house tonight
to see the second play. Kept waiting for Miss Woolf to appear. But
it was so noisy on stage I guess she was afraid to.

Haven't heard so much profanity since Dusty Miller slipped and hit
himself in the crotch with a crow-bar.

If that's the way college professors talk when they're at home no
wonder we have student riots! Thought we might have a slight riot of
our own tonight. But when a couple of our female battleships steamed
up to Father Ignatius to get ammunition, he just smiled quietly and
said it reminded him of an old morality play. They tacked off looking
dazed. I was a little confused myself. Morality play? Maybe Father
Ignatius is getting deaf!

Sunday July 6

As I sat in church today I glanced over at Annie and wondered if she
was thinking what I was—that last Sunday was a lot pleasanter
than this.

Today was very hot and it was Communion Sunday, which means a
longer than usual service.

Ah well, it gave me time to think. I pondered last Sunday's idea of
weather insurance. If I could work it out the policy would guarantee
so many sunny days a year (or summer) and pay off on the bad ones.
Should have great appeal; the bad days pay for the fun you can have
on the good days. Problem is, how do I outguess the weather?

I'm afraid every time I saw a cloud in the sky I'd get heartburn.

Monday July 7

Problem: What will we do with the space at the back of the fire hall when the hospital moves out to its new building?

Answer: Saw Al Pines today. Persuaded him the time had come to stop printing *The Portent* in his basement. Pointed out that there was a building code violation involved. He will rent the space. Bill Dogood will convert his basement to a recreation room and convert the fire hall rooms for printing.

Figure this will pay about $250.00. Not much. But sufficient unto the day. . . .

Tuesday July 8

1)   Remember to see that Al Pines' lease for the fire hall space has a clause in it that gives us the right to evict him if we decide we need the space "in civic interests." Must keep the press beholden.

2)   Remember to give Casey a bottle at Christmas out of that annual case from Bill Dogood. It was his vote that swung the Council, so instead of actually selling that lot to the hospital I was able to get a 99-year lease from them at an annual rent equal to what I paid for it originally (though Casey doesn't know *that*).

All packed for the trip to Toronto in the morning. Annie so excited she kept going to the bathroom all day.

Wednesday July 9

So this is Toronto! Got in about three. By the time we got our hotel rooms and were unpacked, it was five-thirty. Last bus tour left at four. Real shame to miss it, so we walked around a bit on our own.

Naturally, I headed straight away for the city hall. An amazing site. Had trouble convincing Annie that it was all occupied by people employed to run the city. "But what do they all do?" she kept asking as we stared up at floor after floor. How do you explain to someone who doesn't know the business that that isn't a relevant question?

Had dinner at the hotel. Dining room big enough for a lacrosse game. Prices high enough to feed a family for a week back home. Food not as good as Sim Jack's. The waiter called me "Sir"—and made it sound good. Down Upper Upsalquitch way, if someone calls you "Sir" you hit him. Local custom.

Thursday July 10

Left Annie and went off to the first meeting of the Great Lakes–Ontario Probe. Program consisted mostly of government men showing slides and movies of pollution. Had to agree things are pretty messy in these parts. Made some notes. Apparently, it is considered a bad thing here to have your sewage feed right into a river. I had always thought that that was what rivers were for.

This afternoon, they put us all on buses and took us out to see a new sewage treatment plant. Wish I could have taken Annie along; it was very interesting.

Tonight wanted to take Annie to a night club but she had been out shopping all day so after going down to the dining room and spending another family's weekly budget, went back to my room and watched television. Annie is snoring now. Must be the altitude.

Friday July 11

Today, the GLOP people really came to grips with their subject. A couple of college professors presented papers—which they read with all the flare and inflection of Grade Three students. I dozed a bit through that. Then they had a series of workshop sessions, breaking the meeting up into little groups. Being an observer, I felt I didn't belong in all that, so I ducked out to see the insurance company.

Had a little difficulty finding anybody who had ever heard of me. Not very flattering. But, in one way, a bit reassuring. Picked up a lot of good literature I can use to scare people into buying.

Went back to GLOP for the closing speeches.

Saturday July 12

Annie was up with the rooster this morning, raring to go. Yesterday she had discovered the Tourist Bureau. Came away laden with maps and folders on everything in the area.

After fortifying myself with a good breakfast, we went at it. I'll bet we saw more buildings than any Torontonian knows he has! Racked up three museums, an art gallery (nothing in it except some old paintings), a planetarium (all I got out of *that* was a crick in my neck) and two zoos.

As a tourist, I'm a failure. Thank God, it will soon be over and I'll be safely back in Upper Upsalquitch where the tourists stare at *us*!

Sunday July 13

Annie thought it would be nice to go to a big city church today. We asked the doorman to pick one for us. He sent us to the biggest building I've ever seen, church-wise. We were seated by an usher whose pants didn't match his jacket (which had tails). He put us so far from the pulpit that I thought we were watching a puppet show. The minister was wired for sound, and while I could see him bobbing around up there, his *voice* was coming at me out of the ceiling over my head. Very spooky.

Before we left for church, I had called Cousin Ralph and he met us at the hotel for lunch. Getting bald, poor chap. Must be all the pollution in the air up here.

Monday July 14

Today, we took a bus over to see Niagara Falls. It sure does. Annie insisted that we walk across the Peace Bridge to the American side so she could tell her friends she had been in the United States. She bought some postcards there and wanted to mail them on the spot, but I told her she needed American stamps and persuaded her to bring them back to Canada.

On the way back, the bus took us to a park called Queenston Heights, where as I understand it, General Brock (a good guy) drove back the Americans (the bad guys) in the War of 1812. We have since put him up on top of a very high monument and gotten on with the business of persuading Americans to come to Canada when ever they feel like it.

Tuesday July 15

Found out this morning that Annie had never in her life had breakfast in bed. So we ordered some this morning. It arrived sharp at eight, followed by Annie—fully dressed. The scene wasn't quite what I had had in mind. However, we went at it, me under the blankets and her on top of them looking as if she were about to take flight at any moment.

My egg yolk broke when I was trying to get it up off the plate and pop it into my mouth. I jiggled Annie when she was trying to drink her orange juice. The lid fell off the coffee pot into my cup with a splash. Some of the hot coffee hit Annie. She yelped and dropped her toast, buttered side down, on the floor. But the general idea was good. I just hope if we ever do it again she comes more suitably attired. (With a bib.)

Got a great shock when I saw the hotel bill. Naturally, I had charged everything (including the bus trip) to Upper U. Luckily, they let me sign. Joe Azar and I can work out the details later.

Since the plane left at ten (eleven, our time) and we had to drive west for an hour in a bus in order to fly east for two, there wasn't time to try and track down Mr. Girlen as I had planned.

Wednesday July 16

Back in good old Upper Upsalquitch.

My friend Girlen called this morning. Said the company was all set up and ready to go. Asked him what it was called. He said he had wanted to call it "The Upper Upsalquitch Uranium Company" but they couldn't get all that on the stock certificates so they changed it to "World Uranium Corporation."

I said that certainly had a ring to it but wasn't it maybe a little high-sounding for just one hole in New Brunswick.

"Not to worry!" said my friend. I love guys who sit in big city air-conditioned offices and sing "Not to worry!" into the telephone. They should try being on the other end of the line sometime.

Called Al Pines and asked him to attend Council. Later, when I announced the good news, all the councillors except Casey Irving applauded wildly. Casey was too preoccupied figuring out how best to horn in on my venture.

Thursday July 17

Had a tight moment this afternoon. Joe Azar stopped me on the street. Asked how the trip to Toronto went. I realized right away that I should have said something about it at Council last night.

The hotel bill had come in this morning. (They certainly don't waste time!) Gave that to Joe and asked him to take care of it. He glanced at the total and whistled. But I gave him my executive glare and he made no comment except to ask what "M/M" meant before my name up at the top.

"Well," I said, not wanting to get into the matter, "I guess it means 'Mr. Mayor'."

"Um," said Joe. But he could see me building up the executive glare again, so he let it drop. Thank God they didn't spell it right out "Mr. and Mrs."!

Friday July 18

Spent a good part of today writing a piece for *The Portent* on the GLOP meetings. It proved a little harder than I expected to relate the problems of the Great Lakes to the Upsalquitch. But with Annie's help (she's a lot smarter than I let her think she is) I finally got it done.

It will serve to keep interest alive in our sewer project and maybe even soften the screams that are going to go up when they find out what being able to do it indoors is going to cost them. So many of our people are Scottish that I expect there will be a tremendous strain put on the system the day they get their new tax bills.

Saturday July 19

Took my GLOP article over to Al Pines' house. He was busy setting type in the basement. What a messy job! Seemed glad to knock off a spell and chat. Says he'll run the article and write to GLOP for more material.

Turns out he's really quite dedicated to the sewer project. Figures the basement would be a lot drier if it were drained. You hear a lot about the underground press these days, but this is absurd.

Sunday July 20

Was telling the Reverend Angus after church about the one I visited in Toronto. Turns out he attended there when he was in college. Agrees that it's a bit of a barn, but I sensed that in his business the size of the church is a measure of the man running it. A bit like a tycoon proving his wealth by driving a Rolls Royce.

Ministers buck for promotion like anyone else—and getting a big church like that apparently proves you are being extra successful in teaching the humility of Christ.

Monday July 21

Kind of concerned about Annie. She's been mooning a bit lately.
Looking as unsatisfied as the lay of the last minstrel. It bothers me
because I think I know how to cure her but haven't found the courage
yet to try. I'm willing to do my best but at my age you live in fear that
your best won't be good enough.

Talked to Bill Huggins about it once (in an impersonal sort of way).
He said there are a lot of things on the market that are supposed to
help but the only sure-fire thing he knew of was a tongue depressor
and two elastic bands. Sounded silly to me; my tongue isn't the
problem.

Maybe I'll take her for a drive in the car tomorrow to cheer her up.
If Jim Dupuis isn't using it.

Tuesday July 22

Al Pines gave the uranium hunt the headline position in *The Portent*.
He even ran my picture. As soon as people began to get their papers
the telephone started to ring.

I was quite surprised at the reaction. It seemed reasonable to expect
that the voters would be elated at the prospect of being rich. Instead,
most of the calls were from people who thought their flower beds
would be disturbed and/or were afraid of radiation.

Old Grace Adew phoned to tell me she had known about the
uranium for years. She said there was a vein of it running right under
her outhouse, and every time her arthritis bothered her she would go
out and sit there until it was cured. An interesting idea but I couldn't
help thinking prolonged treatments must have been hard on the rest
of her family.

Wednesday July 23

At Council tonight those who had applauded loudest last week were the first to attack the mining survey. Had already called Girlen this morning and told him it was okay to go ahead, so I was in a bit of a spot.

Fortunately, Casey Irving was there and in good form. He pointed out how good it would be for Upper Upsalquitch to have an industry —and how nice it would be for the citizens to be able to pay off their loans and mortgages. Since everybody at the meeting except me owes him money one way or another, this comment had a very healthy effect.

I let it soak for a minute then added that the company was prepared to state in writing that the town would not be all dug up. "After all," I said, "mining is something they do underground. It's not going to effect us up on top." Sure hope I'm right, for they then came around and voted for me to advise Girlen to proceed. Which is good since he arrives in the morning.

Thursday July 24

A whole crew of "surveyors" accompanied Girlen to town today. They looked more like used car salesmen to me. I asked Girlen when the survey would begin. He was kind of vague and said, "Well, first, of course, we have to get the releases signed." Seems they can't go trespassing on people's property without permission, so his men have to go door to door and ask for signatures on release forms.

"That wouldn't be an excuse to sell stock, would it?" I asked. "Of course not!" he cried, looking real hurt. "Well," says I, not believing him for a moment, "be sure you sell my shares first or we may have to hold you and your 'surveyors' for peddling without a license."

Friday July 25

Letty Hinch called this afternoon to say people had been asking her for something on uranium from the library. What should she do? "Tell them we haven't got a thing left," I said. Letty protested. "But we never have had anything!" "Well, then," says I, "you're not lying, are you? Nothing from nothing leaves nothing left, right?" "Well, I guess so," says Letty, sounding unconvinced.

Our seamstress has a very one-track mind. Maybe that's why Bill Huggins sometimes lets her help out at the drug store. I suppose a one-track mentality isn't a bad thing to have around when you're mixing pills. It could be an asset, too, for a librarian. That is, if you had a large number of books to keep track of. In our case, all you have to be able to do is glance down the row and see what's missing.

Saturday July 26

Tonight saw the final performance of our drama festival. Setting aside the financial benefits, am left with the question of whether or not it was good for the town. On the one hand, a lot of folks saw real live drama who might otherwise not have had the opportunity. On the other, they saw it badly performed and, instead of having had their appetites whetted for more, may have been driven back to their TV sets forever.

One man who is certainly happy it's all over is Ned Dervish. Now he can get back to his typical "Snow White Meets King Kong" kind of fare, where what's going on in the audience is more fun to watch than what's on the screen.

Ned was generous enough to suggest throwing a farewell party for the troupe. But his daughter talked him out of it. Said they were a lot of phonies.

Sunday July 27

To my surprise, the Reverend Angus preached a new sermon today.
That means that now he must have fifty-three in his ring binder.
Which may throw him off stride a bit if he's not careful. We may end
up with the Three Wisemen hitting town on New Year's Eve.

Monday July 28

When I was a young and wondering boy, I showed (I thought) some
talent as a poet. Had a few things published in those columns where
newspapers obliged aspiring authors willing to fill the space free-of-
charge. Clipped every poem of mine they ran and pasted it proudly in
a scribbler. Haven't written much poetry since. I wonder why?
Perhaps . . .

> The dreams of youth
> Are but vapours that fade
> And drift away before
> The breeze of age.
>
> The dreams of truth
> Sink into later shade
> Where there is nothing more
> By which to gauge
>
> What is or is not,
> Was or might have been.
> What we once sought
> For now is seen
> As little-value stuff
> And not enough.
>
> And not enough.
>
> Somehow we feel
> There should be something more
> Outside the window
> And beyond the door
> If only we could go and look.
> But searching's ended,
> Roaming's done
> And we make do
> With what we've won.

Tuesday July 29

Dusty Miller and I had a meeting today. The termite business is falling off. Dusty figures it's because he has pretty well covered everybody afraid of bugs and fire.

This affair has worked out so well that now I'm looking for something new that Dusty could sell. Grandpa Heber used to say, "If you've got a good formula, stick with it." What I need is something that is a logical extension of what Dusty's been doing lately and yet is simple enough for him to understand.

Wednesday July 30

Had an idea while shaving this morning. As the day went on, I rehearsed the idea and then sprang it on Council tonight.

What we needed, I said, was what every developing town had—a Building Inspector. I saw Casey Irving flinch so I added quickly that existing buildings like Mr. Irving's houses would not, of course, be affected. However, if a tenant wanted improvements then, of course, the Building Inspector would have to be called in. Since Casey knows Dusty as well as I do, he brightened right away and moved that Dusty be given the new title. All approved.

Thursday July 31

Bless his little heart. Girlen called today to say that all my stock was sold and that he'd be around tomorrow with a cheque. I suggested that cash would do nicely (there being no need to bother Casey Irving with details that don't concern him). Girlen said that was fine by him. Asked him how much he had gotten for the stock. "Two thousand one hundred," he said. Almost dropped the phone. I guess we aren't as accustomed to dealing in big numbers as they are in the big city.

"Is that all right?" he asked, kind of nervous. "Oh yes," I said, "I guess so." "Great then! I'll be in to see you first thing in the morning."

Friday August 1

I will never see August 1st come again without remembering this one. About 10:15 Casey Irving called me—just as I was getting restless over the fact that Girlen hadn't arrived with the money.

"Say," says Casey, keeping his voice down. "I thought you might be interested to know that our friend drew out most of his money last night."

"Oh?" said I carefully, thinking that my request for cash seemed to be making waves.

"Yes," says he, "so I've done a little checking. And do you know what else?" "No," says I, beginning to grope for my *Tums*. "Well, sir," he says, "the whole pack of them, Girlen, surveyors and all have pulled out. I called Fredericton to be sure. They were all on that early morning plane."

So there we are. Girlen has headed back to Toronto where this is the start of Civic Holiday weekend. And I, so far as I can see, am headed for civic disgrace.

Saturday August 2

"You've got to take the bitter with the sweet," as Sim Jack says of his spareribs. Right now I'm pretty well fixed for the bitter. Hardly slept at all last night, thinking about that scoundrel taking off with all that money and not leaving one red cent for me.

Now my mind is focussed on finding the sweet. That is, how am I going to get out of this situation without being tarred and feathered?

Annie in some flutter called after lunch. Said her father was walking around the house grinning and rubbing his hands and muttering things like "That'll fix the old geezer's clock!"

Kind of resented her jumping to the conclusion when he said "old geezer" he meant me, but I let it pass.

"What's happened?" she wanted to know.

"Oh, there's been a little business upset," I said to her and the party line. "Nothing to worry about. I'll tell you Monday."

"Monday?" she asked meaningfully.

"Monday," I replied firmly and went back to biting my nails.

Sunday August 3

Not being quite ready yet to expose myself to the public, skipped church and went for a long walk down the block and back.

Question: What would Grandpa Heber have done in a situation like this? Answer: He'd have skipped town.

No help there. I've got no place to skip to, no other way of making a living than what I'm doing now. And I suspect the market for used mayors isn't too big. So I've got to stay here and see it through.

Tonight, tried to watch TV to get my mind off the problem. Every show seemed to be about crooks and swindlers. Dozed off for a moment and dreamed I was on "This Is Your Life"—wearing handcuffs.

Monday August 4

Today was a holiday. I had proclaimed it so. Ran an ad in *The Portent*. Not that it makes much difference this time of year. Too many of our people are busy helping the tourists run through their money. If ten per cent of those who hire fishing guides here were to catch as many fish as the other ninety per cent claim to have caught, there wouldn't be a minnow left.

And if one per cent found out that most of the "guides" never go fishing themselves, we'd probably have an armed invasion.

Tuesday August 5

The populace is beginning to suspect that all is not uranium that glitters. People are asking me when the survey is going to start. All I can say—and quite honestly, alas, is, "I only know as much as you do."

Called my cousin Ralph today and asked him to check up on Mr. Girlen. He said he would but added, "I can tell you one thing. He must be pretty important. While you've been talking I've been looking in the phone book and he must have one of those private, unlisted numbers because there's no one by that name there."

Wednesday August 6

Ralph called back this afternoon. Mr. Girlen is not in Toronto at the moment. Asked Ralph if he knew where I could reach him. "No," he says, "but if you find out I'll split the reward with you." Seems Mr. Girlen and his "surveyors" have been exploring for uranium all over Canada. The wonder is they didn't hit Upper Upsalquitch sooner.

Called Al Pines and got him over to Council. Got him to bring his camera and shoot a picture of me swearing out a warrant for Mr. Girlen's arrest. Also gambled a little and got Council to put up a reward. Made a speech about how terrible it was that innocent citizens had been victimized in this way. Applause. "You tell 'em, Mayor!" Casey said, looking sad for the camera.

Thursday August 7

Ah well! In times of adversity we must count our blessings.

Item: At least I didn't lose any money on the Girlen fiasco.

Item: I think I gained a few points with the voters over the outcome.

Item: In the fuss, Dusty's appointment as Building Inspector passed without comment. Al Pines merely reported it as one of the recent decisions of Council and let it go at that.

Sooner or later, every owner has to do something to repair or improve his house. I've had Al Pines print up some Building Permit signs. They cost me almost a nickel apiece, which is pretty steep. But Dusty sells them for five dollars and gives me half, so I guess I can't complain.

Friday August 8

Some of the magazines which I subscribed to have begun to arrive. Annie is delighted. I'm kind of pleased, too. There's a lot of interesting stuff in them. I just wish she wouldn't spend so much time with them when she should be working.

However, she came up with a comment today that justifies the whole thing. She looked up from one of them and said, "I keep seeing these ads, 'Keep America Beautiful' and 'Keep Canada Beautiful.' Why can't we do something like that?"

Of course! This is what we need right now! A campaign to spruce up Upper Upsalquitch. The old town could use a little cleaning and the houses, by and large, are pretty shameful. If we could get this going we'd be issuing Building Permits faster than Al could print them.

Saturday August 9

First thing this morning, got ahold of Bill Ellis. With the school not opening for a month, he has lots of time on his hands. Told him about my idea to beautify Upper Upsalquitch. He says he likes it. I said I sort of hoped one of the results we would see was people improving their houses.

"Don't you worry," he assured me, "when the school kids get on the bandwagon there won't be an unaltered house in town." "But there's more to a drive like this than just raising the roof," I protested. "I know that," he says, "but we'll organize survey crews to cover the town. They'll go door to door and make reports on what they find." "Will the Building Inspector get to see those reports?" I asked hopefully. Bill replied, "I suppose so . . . if he wants to." "Oh," I said, "I'm pretty sure he'll want to!"

Sunday August 10

Surprisingly few people in church this morning, even for the middle of August. The choir outnumbered the congregation again. I always feel a bit sorry for the Reverend Angus on a day like this as he looks down at all those empty pews. Sure, he's only doing his job, reading Sermon Thirty-Two from his ring binder. But a good minister is an artist and needs an appreciative audience. Have always felt that the custom of not applauding in church was a bad thing—for the minister and for his religion.

Another change I'd like to make is to have the collection plate at the door. I always get nervous when I see it coming. And that spoils my mood.

Monday August 11

Old J. C. Hanson popped off this morning. Very nice timing! All I have to do in a case like this is write a letter to the insurance company, dated last Friday, enclosing a cheque prepaying his premiums for a year. Tomorrow (or whenever the relatives bring it up) I'll report his departure.

In due course, a cheque will come in for the full amount of the policy plus the unused balance of the money I sent them today. While the cheque is made out to the person he named (his daughter, in this case) it comes to me for delivery. I take it to the person named, explain that to protect the deceased I had prepaid the insurance just before he died—and collect a cheque for that amount. It works every time—and saves me the embarrassment of a lot of explanation about monthly versus annual payments.

Tuesday August 12

The Portent's picture of me swearing out the warrant for Girlen's arrest brought another spate of phone calls: people who had bought shares and now were wondering what they should do. All I could say to each of them was that the matter is in the hands of the police, but that even if the dastardly swindlers are caught, it is doubtful whether they will ever see their money again.

I couldn't help adding that if they had put their money into insurance it would still be there and growing for them. A couple expressed interest in the idea. I'll have to get busy and follow them up. There must be more money in this town than I thought!

Wednesday August 13

Was almost late for Council meeting tonight. Fellow dropped in to see me and we got talking. He's a writer collecting stories about New Brunswick's past.

Told me he's just been over at Tabusintac, out past Neguac, looking for a rock. Seems that is where the Mohawks and Micmacs are supposed to have ended what was known as "The Mohawk War." Back in those days they had a very sensible system for fighting a war: the chiefs of the two parties met in single combat. In this case, after a long struggle the Micmac chief got the upper hand, forced the Mohawk back and squashed him on a big boulder on the shore. End of war.

The government would like to identify the stone now as a historical sight. It's a little late to start looking. The fellow asked if we had any spots around our town that should be written up. Had to admit that I couldn't think of anything very startling that had happened around here. Sent him off to see Al Pines who is the closest thing we have to a local historian.

As I bustled over to Council, thought how smart those Indians were and how few wars we'd have today if we played it their way and insisted that the chiefs do the fighting. Give us six months of that and they'd be turning the Pentagon into squash courts.

Thursday August 14

At last night's Council meeting mentioned casually that Bill Ellis was thinking of organizing the high school kids in a drive to make Upper Upsalquitch an even more beautiful place to live in. Everyone agreed the program should be encouraged.

Bill Huggins made some comment about the kids starting by cleaning up themselves. But no one followed this up; it is pretty generally known that Bill has a piece of Clipper Hill's tonsorial business. Every haircut is money in the bank for him.

Personally, I see nothing wrong with long hair. After all, if it hadn't been for people with long hair the New Testament would never have been written.

Friday August 15

As I listened to myself today talking to some of the folks in Sim Jack's at morning coffee time, I marvelled at how easily I have fallen into a sort of "mayor lingo" over the years. I trot out platitudes like a dealer shuffling cards. No matter what you say, automatically I produce a safe, conservative response that sounds as though either I am agreeing with you or would agree with you if I could speak freely and not as the Mayor. In neither case do I say anything that, five minutes later, could be quoted to anyone as proof that I was favourable toward anything.

I guess I should be ashamed of being like that. But, in truth, evasiveness becomes a way of life—and finding new ways of being strongly and forcefully neutral is part of politics. It is one of the minor joys of the job. I have always made it clear that I am willing to take a position on anything. I just never make clear what the position is.

Saturday August 16

One of our tourists left a copy of last weekend's *Boston Globe* in our "Tourist Attraction." Found it when I made my weekly inspection trip today. It wasn't all there (we sometimes run out of paper) but I took home what was left. Read an interesting article about the zoo in Boston. (I think they call it the Yard.) Apparently it attracts a lot of people.

Maybe *we* should have a zoo, too. At the moment, all we have to offer visitors is our Tourist Attraction and Auntie Maude's place out on the Back Road. We have a sign up pointing the way to the Tourist Attraction but, so far, Auntie Maude's merits have always been able to speak for themselves.

Sunday August 17

By coincidence, the topic the Reverend Angus had decided to share with us today (Sermon #33) was Noah and his Ark. Pointed out in a very modern way that while the animals went in two by two, there were probably a few more got off the boat than got on. Guess that makes Noah the first man to have bred his cast upon the waters.

Anyway, it all set me thinking some more about having a zoo. This afternoon called Cousin Ralph and told him what I was considering. His first comment was that he knew an old goat that should be in a cage. Asked him to find out for me who to contact for used animals. We'll have to start simply and work up. I don't think the local citizens will go for spending too much on this.

Monday August 18

Cousin Ralph called back this afternoon to say he had telephoned various zoos and had been told they have no animals to spare. Too bad. I had thought maybe if one of their lions or something was coming up for retirement, Upper Upsalquitch might be a nice place for him to end his days.

Tuesday August 19

Amazing how things fall in place! A travelling salesman came into Sim Jack's this morning. In the course of conversation he said he'd been in Moncton yesterday and had gone to the circus last night.

"A real genuine circus, with animal acts and everything?" I asked. "Sure thing! Just like when we were kids. Lions, elephants, monkeys. The whole bit. Kind of sad, though."

I nodded to Sim Jack to pour him some more coffee. "Why's that?"

"Well, they don't get crowds like they used to. I heard afterwards that they're almost broke. One more booking like that and they'll be bankrupt."

Wednesday August 20

Had some pretty dramatic news for Council tonight: the circus is coming to town! They'll arrive late Saturday night, set up their tents and give us a big parade at noon on Sunday. (Reverend Angus and Father Ignatius had better plan to cut it short that day!)

The Councillors were pretty excited. Nearest thing we've ever had to a circus was a little show Auntie Maude used to put on for the boys. Wasn't quite the same thing, although I understand there *was* a dog and a pony involved. (That's the curse of being Mayor; a lot of fun is hearsay!)

Casey was the only one who looked sceptical. "Why are they coming here?" he demanded. "A circus has to pull crowds to make money. There aren't enough people in this town to fill a circus tent for one night. How do we know they won't go broke?"

"Well," I admitted, "that possibility does exist."

Thursday August 21

The advance agent for the circus showed up today. Came right to see me. (I had promised full cooperation on the phone.) Took him to Sim Jack's for coffee. But he was restless and wanted to get going. As we came out, he said, "Well, let's go downtown and slap up some posters." I said, "This *is* downtown!" and he turned sort of green. However, he finally went off to do what he could and I called Milky Becker and told him to give the agent a day and then arrest him for defamation of property.

Friday August 22

Milky called this afternoon to say he had arrested the agent and the agent wasn't very happy about it. "He says he wants a lawyer."

"What did you tell him?"

"I told him we don't have any lawyers in Upper Upsalquitch."

"Well, that's the truth. What have you done with him?"

"I've got him in the fire hall, handcuffed to the pumper. If there's a fire, I sure hope he can run fast!"

I thought about the problem for a moment. "Look, Milky," I says, "the thing is that until the circus gets here, we've got to hold him *incommunicado.*"

"Where's that?" asks Milky.

"Well, what about your basement?"

"O.K.," says Milky, doubtfully, "but I don't think my wife is going to like it."

"Oh," says I, reassuringly, "it'll be nice for her to have a man around the house."

Saturday August 23

The circus came to town today. Late this evening the owner phoned me. "Well," he says, "we've got our tents up and everything is pretty well in place. But I've got a problem. I've been looking all over town for our advance agent. I see his posters are up but I can't find him."

"That's easy," I said. "He's in jail."

"He's in what?" screams the owner. "What did he do?"

"He was defaming property, that's what," I says, real stern like. "You said nothing to me on the phone about plastering our town with sheets of sticky paper. He's made a mess."

I didn't catch all the owner said at this point but it didn't sound nice. Finally, he asked, "All right, how do we get him out?"

"Just by paying his fine. Two hundred dollars." There was what sounded like a death rattle on the other end of the line and then he finally says, "Well, it serves him right. Let's leave him there for awhile."

Sunday August 24

The circus parade today was pretty. Not a big one, and the equipment and performers all need a new paint job. However, all the town turned out to see it and had a good time. And, after all, that's what matters most.

Every Sunday the Reverend Angus tells the children in the congregation a little story. Today he tried to tie in with our event by telling them about the old Roman circus and how they used to throw Christians to the lions. Things have improved somewhat since those days; now the minister throws lines to the Christians.

It *was* very good of him to give us what was, in effect, a commercial.

Monday August 25

The location for the circus may not be the best but it had to be. Council has bought Pres Philhower's farm to make it into our sewage plant. (And Pres has paid me to let go of my option.) It seemed the logical place since we own it. But it's not very attractive. (Pres was never much of a farmer; he didn't seem to notice things like stumps and stones.)

Went out this afternoon and said a few nice words to the audience for the first show. Gave me a chance to look at the animals. A lion, an elephant, a couple of striped mules they swear are zebras, two monkeys, and something that I suspect was once somebody's sheep dog but now has its hair cut all funny and is labelled "African baboon hunter."

Tuesday August 26

The circus put on two shows yesterday and two today. I showed up
again for today's evening performance. It was kind of sad. The
mosquitoes didn't have enough people to go around. The owner
buttonholed me afterwards, looking pretty worried. "Where is
everybody?" he asked.

"That *is* everybody," I replied. "And I must compliment you.
They've all enjoyed it."

"Enjoyed it, hell," he cried. "We're losing our shirts!"

"Oh now," I reassured him, "I'm sure everything will come out
right. After you've paid the property rent you'll still have a nice profit."

"Property rent!" he screamed. "What property rent?"

I explained that the town always charged for the use of its land.
"But don't worry," I says, "it's only a thousand dollars for the whole
week." He went into a sort of fit but I had to leave before I could see
the end of it.

Wednesday August 27

The Councillors were right on my tail going into the meeting tonight.
Casey Irving asked the question I was expecting. Before I could get a
grip on my gavel he demanded, "What happened?" We all knew what
he meant.

During the night the circus had disappeared. Gone. Tents, wagons,
calliope and all. Well, not quite all. The advance agent was still handcuffed to Milky Becker's furnace and Milky, who had been waiting
with our special deputy Dusty Miller, had stopped the exodus at the
farm gate long enough to take their animals into custody as security
against the rent.

Since it didn't seem likely the circus would be playing many dates
with neither advance advertising nor animals, I said I felt our chances
of collecting were pretty poor.

"Well, then," demanded Casey, "what are we going to do with those
animals?"

"Do?" I replied. "Why, we're going to have a zoo, that's what. A
real tourist attraction!"

Thursday August 28

We let the advance agent go this afternoon. Knowing the circus had headed west, Milky took the liberty of leaving him on the eastbound side of the highway. It really didn't seem to make much difference to the agent; he was more interested in getting away than in where he was going.

Not a bad fellow, really. Like so many people in the world he was simply a victim of forces larger than himself.

Friday August 29

Interesting problem in economics has arisen. The animals seem happy enough in their cages—I guess they've been in them a long time—but they consume an awful lot of food. Must admit (but only to myself) that I hadn't thought about that.

I'd seen pictures of kids feeding peanuts to elephants. But it had never occurred to me that without a square meal beforehand that little bag of peanuts is not quite enough.

Sim Jack is contributing all his table scraps but that hardly satisfies any species. Have put Dusty in charge of the problem. As a matter of fact, I have put him in charge of *both* problems; not only do they eat a lot, there's the problem at the other end.

Saturday August 30

I'm a very proud man today. Dan Prosser's wife is a bit of an artist so I got her sign painting. Effective today, when you enter Upper Upsalquitch from either direction you are greeted by a big sign that says ZOO.

I'll bet there's not another town within 5,000 miles that has a sign saying *that* at its entrance!

I was downtown this afternoon when a car coming from one direction stopped beside another coming from the opposite. "Where's the zoo?" one driver called. "I don't know," yelled the other looking around. "Maybe this is it!"

I started over to give directions but both drivers looked at me coming and drove off. Guess they'd never seen plus-fours before.

Sunday August 31

Al Pines' wife is now superintendent of our Sunday School. A fine woman. It being a nice day, she held Sunday School out at the zoo. To teach the value of Christian sharing, she got each child to bring food for the animals. It was just as well because Dusty went on a toot last night and never did show up to feed them.

That sort of thing doesn't bother him much, apparently. As he said when I finally roused him this afternoon, "Well, Mayor, I look at it this way: the less I feed them, the less I have to shovel."

I told him he'd better keep feeding and shovelling because if that elephant dies on him he'll *really* have to do some shovelling!

Monday September 1

Labour Day! In England and Wales they call it a "Bank Holiday."
Neither term means much to us. For most of us, the bank could be on
a holiday most of each month. And labour is a dirty word to most of
my voters anyway. But the kids like it because it stalls the starting
of school for another day.

Tuesday September 2

Many of our voters still have an affection for things British. Occurred
to me that since we have a lion we should try to get that other animal
that's always shown supporting the Royal Arms: the unicorn.

Haven't seen any around here, so I wrote two weeks ago to London,
England. So far, no reply. Perhaps the letter was wrongly addressed.
Information is so hard to get here! Vaguely remembered that their zoo
is called "Hyde Park" so I sent my request there. Addressed it to "The
Director," whose name I believe is Dr. Jekyll. If I don't hear soon
will write again.

Wednesday September 3

True to his word, Bill Ellis started off the high school year by announcing that as a fall project, the school would undertake to "Upgrade Upper Upsalquitch". The Student Council will appoint committees and get things going.

All this I learned from his phone call this morning. He wanted me to appear at assembly next week and commend them. I suggested with modesty that it might be better to save the Mayor's praise for a later date. However, I promised to send him a statement *he* could read to them, saying that the Mayor and Council wish them well.

(It is important that this project remain Bill's, or the kids', idea.) What matters the glory so long as our fair town is made more beautiful?

Thursday September 4

Work is about to start on our sewage disposal plant and until we get everything set up properly, we'll have to locate the animals and the zoo somewhere else. (They can go back once the earth is over the tile.)

Told Al Pines about our problem and he offered to run a free ad asking people to take them in as temporary pets. I don't know. I can see the monkeys going fast and maybe the striped mules (Letty Hinch actually believes they're zebras), but the African baboon hunter is kind of touchy (can't say I blame him) and the lion and elephant are a bit on the large side for any family's food budget.

Thanked Al but told him we'd try to work it out some other way first.

Friday September 5

It's amazing where good ideas come from! Got one today right off the top of my head. Went to get a haircut and was telling Clipper Hill about the problem of having to move the animals.

He snipped away in silence for a while and then he says, "Those cage wagons are pretty heavy."

"Yes," I said, "and we haven't got a tractor or anything to pull them."

"Right!" cried Clipper, waving his shears in dangerous excitement (I was glad he wasn't shaving me), "but you do have an elephant! That's what they use them for in India; to pull things!"

Brilliant. I was so excited I almost felt like paying him—but I recaptured my dignity in time.

Saturday September 6

Got ahold of Dan Prosser today, figuring it was time he got into the zoo act. Told him he was the committee (of one) to work out how to harness an elephant.

"Oh, I can tell you that on the phone," he said, trying to get off easily, "same as a horse."

"Fine," I replied. "Now you know what your committee target is: to find some harness that's big enough." He squirmed a bit but finally hung up. Figure anybody in town that has some rope around had better lock it up. Dan is a very resourceful fellow.

Sunday September 7

Our girls' softball team was in the county playoff this afternoon. Naturally, I had to show up for so important an event, even though my interests do not lie in the sport as much as the participants.

It was kind of intriguing to watch the crowd. The other team was from Robinsonville. Their fans came streaming into town in as great a variety of vehicles as I've ever seen.

What made it especially interesting for me was their reaction to our team. Joe Azar is the coach and has our girls outfitted in pretty attractive uniforms. Their shorts are about as short as shorts can get without the girls being short of shorts. The Robinsonville girls wore regulation baseball pants (like my plus fours). The umpire behind the pitcher was from Robinsonville. He let three of our girls steal bases just watching them slide.

We beat our opponents 12 to 3—a very satisfactory margin.

Monday September 8

Problems, problems! Was any man ever more beset with them? You try to do good, to be a good Mayor—and all you get is problems. Turns out that the farm we bought for our sewage disposal plant has only a foot of earth. From there on down to China it's solid rock. No way you can bury anything—unless you blast. Now (problems, problems!) what can I do with all that rock?

Tuesday September 9

Still no reply from Hyde Park Zoo about a unicorn. If Good Queen Bess were still alive I'd write her. I'll bet she knew where to hunt for one! Well, I'll give it another week. Perhaps Dr. Jekyll is away or out of sorts.

Meantime, the animals seem to be prospering. Dusty is looking a little tired these days. He says the shovelling part of the job is what is getting him, especially shovelling for the elephant.

I tried to inspire him by reminding him of the wonderful roses we're going to have next year as a result. He says, "If that elephant doesn't quit piling it up all over the place we won't have room for roses!"

Wednesday September 10

Dan Prosser slipped me the word at Council tonight; he has found a way to harness the elephant. I gather a couple of farmers may find it a little hard to hoist hay into their lofts until we're through but, after all, the greater good must be served.

Since, with a little pressure, Dusty has become a pretty competent elephant driver, it looks as though we'll be all set when the time comes.

Dusty is getting a mite touchy. The boys at the Legion Hall who used to kid him when he became Termite Inspector have now switched their attention to his clean-up duties at the zoo. Some of their comments are pretty funny—but that's my opinion, not his!

Thursday September 11

Wrote again to London about where to look for a unicorn. This time, tried a new address. The've got a guy over there that I've read about who should really know a lot about animals; the Keeper of the Privy Seal.

Wrote to him in care of Buckingham Palace which is where I expect he works, unless the Queen takes her seal with her when she travels. I've never noticed it in any pictures.

Friday September 12

Had an idea while I was shaving. Called Clare Latrouche and asked her to be Chairlady of the Upgrade Upper Upsalquitch Adult Committee. She asked who the members were. Since I had just made up the name of the Committee, I told her I respected her judgement; she could select whomever she wanted.

Then she asked what the Committee was supposed to do. I said it seemed to me the first thing was to beautify the approach to Upper Upsalquitch. Maybe what we needed on each side of the road was a long rock garden.

She said, "Where could we possibly get enough rocks for all that?" So I made a reasonable suggestion.

Saturday September 13

A beautiful early fall day. The leaves haven't started to turn yet, but there is a clean crispness to the air. Since Jim Dupuis didn't have a funeral booked, I put Annie in the car and took her for a drive. She had only one request; to avoid the zoo. I gather she doesn't entirely share my enthusiasm for our new asset.

However, she did have a good idea. When I told her how afraid I was that the blasting of the rock farm would upset the animals, she suggested we have a parade. "Declare it Animal Day," she suggested. "The elephant can pull the wagons and we'll get the Elks and Moose from Upsalquitch to march behind."

"Well, not right behind," I said cautiously. "I think it might be a good idea to have Dusty with a wheelbarrow and a shovel right behind."

Sunday September 14

While the Reverend Angus was holding forth this morning, my mind wandered. Found myself wishing that I could be a better mayor. I know that I lack dignity and good bearing. And I lack the colour and wit one senses in reports of mayors in larger communities.

What I wouldn't give to have the charisma and attraction of a man like Camillien Houde—that wonderful, fat, French character Montreal had for a mayor off and on around the Second World War! Other mayors still exchange stories about him.

I would never have dared accept an invitation to an English-speaking city to kick off a football game and say, "It is a great pleasure to come here to kick off this ball. I would be happy anytime to come back and kick all your balls off!"

Everybody laughed and said, "That's Houde!" I would have gotten lynched.

Monday September 15

Casey Irving told me today that he is about to build a new house.
I think he is smart to sort of pass the word around before he starts.
Lets people get used to the idea. A bank man has to be careful about
how he spends his money. People are apt to suspect it's theirs.

Naturally, I called Dusty right away and told him to hike over there
with a building permit and a termite policy. And I made a note on my
calendar to catch him on fire and theft later.

Sounds like it's going to be a nice place. Out on that bump of land
by the river. Probably the best spot around. I've heard of others who
are talking of building there. If enough people like Casey do it—those
people with pull—we'll call it Knob Hill.

Tuesday September 16

A woman out on the Back Road phoned me today all upset. A couple
of high school kids had come to her door and told her she should get
rid of her privy. I guessed right away it was an Upgrade team, so I
explained it to her. But she was still upset.

"If I don't get rid of it, people will think I don't care about our
town, but if I do get rid of it where will I go?"

I suggested that a lot of people had them indoors now. "That's
disgusting!" she exclaimed. "And very unsanitary, too."

"But these are flush toilets," I explained. "You push down on a
lever and it's all flushed away."

"What happens if something falls in?" she demanded. "Last month
my upper plate fell in. If I had flushed it away, I would have had to
buy a new one!"

"Well," I suggested lamely, "perhaps, in your case, you should take
out your teeth before you go to the bathroom."

Wednesday September 17

Election Day in Canada. The day when men who have two drinks a year moan because the bars are closed.

Because of the time zones the results are still incomplete but I see no reason why I shouldn't sleep well. That other party is going to be defeated again—which only goes to prove that the public has not yet gone completely mad.

Come to think of it, Canadians have always behaved pretty well. Guess we're just plain more intelligent than some. We keep our animals off campaign posters and locked in the zoo.

Thursday September 18

The results of yesterday's national election were very satisfactory. Our party has a comfortable majority. And that sterling citizen—the man whose hobby is trying to become the father of his country— the prolific Ferdinand Leboeuf swept our riding clean. So, it's back to Ottawa and bottom pinching for him. They'll probably make him Minister of Labour.

Friday September 19

Was very flattered. Ferdinand Leboeuf dropped in this afternoon to thank me for my help in the election. He is all hot-eyed and raring to go. Parliament doesn't open for a couple of weeks but he says he's going to go up to Ottawa now and get to work. Surely no man was ever more eager to serve his country. Service is his motto.

We've made a little deal on government contracts that may pay off sometime. Nothing dishonest, though. It is the duty of the elected member to keep the voters advised on what is going on in the capital. All I asked of Leboeuf is that he advise me in advance.

Saturday September 20

Had Dusty Miller put on the storm windows today. It may be a bit early but it has been my experience that most people keep postponing it. Then, suddenly, there comes a cold spell and everyone starts shouting for Dusty to give them a hand. If I wanted mine put on then, I'd probably have to pay him.

As it is, he's quite willing to do it out of friendship. I keep an eye on him and whenever I sense he's beginning to tire a bit, I go out and chat for a while. Tell him I hear there's a vacancy coming up on the Council soon. Things like that.

What with having to wash them all first and take down the screens it takes him most of the day. By the time he's through I feel exhausted. But these chores have to be faced. I always say, "Never put off 'til tomorrow what you can get done for you today."

Sunday September 21

My customary Sunday morning mid-sermon reverie today was on marriage. I will admit there have been times when I have toyed with the idea of trying it, but I have now been a benedict so long that I no longer have to take cold showers.

Besides I have never been convinced that marriage guarantees happiness. It seems to me that marriage is to love as a hernia is to pole vaulting.

I know what Annie has in mind. If she tries to needle me she may run into a snarl.

Monday September 22

The high school students are continuing their door-to-door survey. One smart thing they're offering to do is gardening where it's needed. They charge a nominal rate with the proceeds for charity. Will have to keep an eye on this. If the fund builds up to any worthwhile size I will have a suggestion to make.

Now if Clare Latrouche gets her Adult Committee going and we get those rocks moved, maybe I can persuade Council to put up some money to pay the high school kids to help with the planting.

Have always wanted a gate to the town; pillars of stone and a sign across the road that says "Welcome to Upper Upsalquitch." Had Dusty work on it one time. He figured we'd either need a four lane highway or newsprint-size type to get all that on the sign. Looks as though I'll have to compromise. Maybe we could use Brigham Young's line and just have it read "This is the place."

Tuesday September 23

Finally got a reply from England today! A very nice letter from that guy who takes care of the seal. Said he was sorry but he did not know of any unicorns that might be available at the moment. However, he said, if he ever saw one I would be the first to know.

Wednesday September 24

Overheard Casey talking about his new house before Council met tonight. Got to wondering whether the Mayor shouldn't be planning to move to Knob Hill as well. The leader of the people deserves the best. Yet there is merit in modesty; the less attention you attract the fewer questions are asked.

This present house is all paid for and, thanks to my frugal life style, the cost of maintenance is low. (That's why, for example, the roof right now is the same color as the new one on the school.) If I were to build another house people might wonder how an unsalaried mayor could afford it.

I think that here I have the best of all possible worlds, being loved, respected—and left alone.

Thursday September 25

The sewer pipes in town are all laid and the new sod is in place over them. (Didn't make much on the sod. The boys weren't very careful how they stripped it at the sewage farm. A lot of waste.)

Just hope and pray no one goes out to inspect the end of the line until we get the sewage plant working. Some finnicky person might make a fuss if they found out that at present it is all running back into the Upsalquitch.

But after all, it is a big river and it is their sewage. It's not as if those that get their water from the river were dealing with strangers.

Friday September 26

Today's mail brought a form letter and a bunch of pamphlets from a group all charged up about drug abuse. That's progress for you! When I was a boy the concern was self abuse. Looks as though the Affluent Society has gotten our minds on higher things.

This group wants all us mayors to get behind their drive to educate young people on the evils of narcotics. There's no way I'm going to help though. So far, we haven't had any trouble here. If I stand up and start spouting off about "pot" and LSD and all that, every kid in town will start wondering what it's really like to try them.

Saturday September 27

Damnation! Al Pines called this morning and I'm still boiling. Those dopes who sent me the mailing yesterday also sent a letter to the paper saying that the Mayor was being asked to cooperate. A dirty trick. Naturally, Al wanted to know what I was going to do.

With visions of a headline that said "Mayor Refuses to Fight Drug Abuse," I explained slowly and carefully how I felt. Al said he understood my position but he thought he'd talk to a few school kids to see how they look at it. And away we go!

Sunday September 28

After mulling it over during the Reverend Angus' doubtless excellent sermon on Moses in the bullrushes, went over to see Al, explained again how I felt and asked him straight out to lay off. He refused.

I was so angry I could have hit him, but restrained myself in time. His is the only paper in town and the town election isn't that far away. But I did go so far as to say something about the freedom of the press not including the right to make trouble where none exists. Al just grinned and said, "When it comes to making much out of nothing, you're no innocent yourself, Mayor!" Hah! Wonder what he meant by that?

Monday September 29

Had an idea while shaving. For some time have been concerned about the lack of books in our library. Books are expensive. They would eat into the Carnegie grant pretty fast if I wasn't careful. Last night I read a mailing piece offering condensed books. Each volume contains a whole whack of novels. If we were to subscribe, we'd be able to count each novel as a book. Before long we'd have an impressive number to report. And the bindings would look real good on the shelf.

The cost isn't much. Maybe I can get one of the Councillors to buy a subscription as a gift to the town. Bill Huggins has that new bench we gave him for outside his store now. I'll see him. Of course he'd get to read the books first, too. After me.

Tuesday September 30

Those nervy kids! Two high school brats showed up at my door this morning doing their "Upgrade Upper Upsalquitch" survey. Said that they had looked my place over and thought it would be nice if I had it painted. They don't realize that painting costs money. Had to be polite, of course. But unless I can figure how to get my hands on some paint and find a painter who is behind in his taxes, this is one house they're not going to Upgrade no matter what!

Wednesday October 1

Al Pines came by tonight to cover the Council meeting. Since he didn't seem to be harbouring any bad feelings about our session on Sunday, I asked him if he had interviewed any kids yet.

He said, "No. I've been thinking over what you said and I've decided to shelve the whole issue for now."

Clapped him on the back and told him I admired his judgement. Bill Huggins saw us talking and winked at me. Bill's drugstore is one of Al's biggest advertisers. When I saw Bill on Monday morning and explained my problem he must have called Al right away. Thank goodness there is someone in town with a sense of justice!

Thursday October 2

Problem: A new man arrived in town last week. A mutual fund salesman. Rented some space from Sim Jack, next to the laundry (the old bicycle shop). He has been looking for a secretary and had the nerve to call up Annie.

She told me right away, all upset because he offers real money. Told her not to worry, that if she wanted the job I certainly wouldn't stand in her way. She sounded grateful for the understanding.

Answer: Called the RCMP. Asked them to investigate the man immediately. Then got Al Pines to report in *The Portent* (front page) that the RCMP was investigating him. No one in town will touch him with a ten foot pole. He'll move on in a week.

Friday October 3

Before I climb into bed tonight I'm going to stand at attention. My national sentiments aren't as strong as they should be. Certainly am a poor man to be running a town full of United Empire Loyalists. But the fact is that tomorrow, which begins shortly, is the anniversary of the death of Henry Carey.

All over the world, people sing variations of "God Save the King." I'll wager none of them know that it was first offered as a number in musical shows. Long after Carey was dead, it finally surpassed his other famous number "Sally In Our Alley."

Strange how men can leave their mark on the world in unexpected ways! George M. Cohan, the American song writer: will his rousing war songs someday become national anthems? Nothing much really wrong with "It's a Grand Old Flag."

And the Mayor of Upper Upsalquitch; what will he be remembered for? Probably for being a nut—if someone looks in and sees me standing at attention by my bed.

Saturday October 4

Couldn't get to sleep last night thinking about what would happen if I lost the election. Am now facing the realization that if I became ex-Mayor I would also become ex-Annie.

Called her up today and took her for a drive. Reminded her that an election wasn't far off. Found it suspicious that she asked who I thought might be running against me. As I mentioned a few names I watched her face. She didn't even flinch at Sim Jack. What perverse creatures women are! Thank God I never married!

Sunday October 5

The Reverend Angus hung his sermon today on that line from Milton "They also serve who only stand and wait." As soon as I heard it my mind jumped to the election. I certainly am willing to serve. The tough part is having to wait; that's what I can't stand.

Suddenly thought, "What if Sim Jack did decide to run for Mayor?" He's pretty well known. A picture of Annie and Sim crossed my mind and I got so charged up I groaned out loud. Several people looked at me, so I had to nod my head at the Reverend Angus as if I had been reflecting on some point they had missed.

I've got to do something soon—Milton notwithstanding, I cannot wait.

Monday October 6

Had an idea while shaving this morning. I find campaigning very wearing—and I don't like the risk of something going wrong. Even though Election Day isn't for awhile, I'm starting to worry.

Then, this morning I had this great idea! Wouldn't it be wonderful if fair Upper Upsalquitch were to become the first place in the world to elect a *Mayor For Life*!

After all, we have Senators who last almost forever. And those pocket-pickers in the civil service never get fired. Why should a Mayor have to stick his neck out every second year?

I think this must be the greatest idea I have ever had. But it's going to require a little arranging.

Tuesday October 7

Dusty and I went over the Building Permits book today. We're not doing too badly. He has learned that the Termite Insurance can be worked in very nicely when he's inspecting jobs in progress. The high school kids are working away—and even Clare Latrouche's committee has stirred up some business.

Trouble is, we're starting to run into cold weather and it's getting hard to persuade people to, say, tear out an exterior wall that needs replacing.

Looks as though we'll have to ease off until Spring. I'll have to find Dusty an inside sport. Would love to give him another title, but three might be a bit thick. Can a Termite Inspector be a Building Inspector and also, say, a Plumbing Inspector? I doubt it. Perhaps I'll have to find a new man; someone in the flush of youth who is plumb eager to get into a joint effort.

Wednesday October 8

Had a call from the Mounties today. As a result, was able to report to Council tonight that that swindler Girlen had been caught. In a way, it was an act of God.

Canada has always been plagued by having too many places called "Saint John." Apparently Mr. Girlen got confused and contacted the mayor of a Saint John where he had been before instead of one he wanted to survey. Said mayor called the RCMP—and that was it.

The Mounties wanted to know if I would testify but I begged off. Girlen will go to jail without my help and I see no point in getting into a courtroom discussion about who got taken for what.

Thursday October 9

They finally got around to blasting out at the sewage plant site. Shook every window in town every time they set off a charge. Drove out with Annie tonight to see how it was going. They certainly stirred things up!

It was unfortunate that the weeping tile had all been delivered to the site before the blasting started. I wonder what we can get for ten truck loads of broken tile?

As Annie and I stood surveying the piles of rubble, fellow pulled up in a car with a foreign license. Asked what was going on. Told him we were getting ready to lay sewage tile. He glanced around, shook his head and said, "You sure must have a big house!"

Now, maybe he just was trying to be funny. But when I told him it was for the whole town, he looked at me as if I were crazy, shook his head again and drove off. Perhaps we *should* check the figures.

Friday October 10

Clare Latrouche called in tears this afternoon. The trucks have begun carting rock from the sewage plant out to the edge of town for her committee's rock garden.

She said she had heard the rock would be moved today so she had her committee out on the site bright and early, all ready to arrange the stones prettily. "You've got to stop them!" she sobbed. "They keep coming and coming! Load after load of jagged boulders. And they're just dumping them anywhere. Some of the piles are eight feet high. Two of my members have quit already. What am I going to do?"

Tried to cheer her up by telling her we were going to end up with the biggest and best rock garden in Canada. "Well, it will certainly be the biggest," she sniffed. Promised I'd get a couple of men out there to do the rough work. Ah me! Nobody knows the rubble I've seen!

142

Saturday October 11

The parade we had on Thursday wasn't much of a success. The Elks and the Moose from Upsalquitch refused to march. Jealousy, probably. And Dusty wouldn't wear a funny hat. As a matter of fact, he refused to push a wheelbarrow, but for a very logical reason. "I can't steer the elephant and be back behind shovelling up, too," he pointed out. "Suppose he lets go on a turn? There's no such thing as a backseat driver for an elephant!"

As it was, the elephant was quite well behaved and where he did let go, the homeowners were quick to remove the evidence. Around here it's become a form of one-upmanship to have fresh elephant fertilizer on flower beds.

By the time the parade was over the blasting was done.

Sunday October 12

Bill Huggins has his stock of new diaries in, so I stopped by yesterday to pick up one of the old ones before he threw them out. Can't see much point in buying a new one when all that's wrong with the old ones is the date.

Flicking through it this morning before putting it away until January, I noticed that today is Columbus Day, the anniversary of when old Christopher was supposed to have reached the American continent. I'll bet he'd never recognize it now! It has become sort of incontinent.

Back in those days, about the worst thing going on was a little tobacco smoking down south. Today, there's puffery all over the place. You wonder why he bothered to come. As it was, he put in a lot of hard days, scared the hell out of the Indians and, in the end, had nothing to show for it but his Christopher medal.

Monday October 13

Thanksgiving Day up here. Must confuse our American friends, ours being early. We've moved the date around a bit. Used to coincide with Armistice Day; then it matched the American date for a while. Then President Roosevelt moved theirs closer to Christmas to perk up business, and we moved ours back because it was too *close* to Christmas. Ambassador Joe Kennedy wanted to move theirs again to commemorate the end of Prohibition. We stood fast; Prohibition's end was a sad day for a lot of us, especially if you had a still near the U.S. border.

Since '57, ours has stayed the second Monday in October. The Americans celebrate the first harvest of their Pilgrim Fathers and the liberty to worship as they wish. We just go around being generally thankful.

A pretty quiet day. School closed, bank closed. A lot of the men out in the woods doing a little hunting. I just sat around, thinking. Mostly about how to be sure of re-election.

Well, I guess sometimes a leader has to do things in the best interests of his followers that they themselves would hesitate to do. Having made up my mind on what is best for them, I have no other course than to forge ahead. Since Casey has indicated that he wants to be Mayor next, I guess he's my first target. But gently!

Tuesday October 14

An interesting problem is developing. And the Councillors are getting a bit edgy about it.

Clipper Hill had a salesman in to see him before the holiday. Result: Clipper is now the official agent in these parts for *Torrie Wigs*.

Clipper's barber shop is the only one for miles, so he's got us by the long hairs. Now, with all those wigs the salesman sold him standing around on plastic heads, the place looks like a beauty parlor. Makes the boys uncomfortable.

Worse than that, Clipper has started working on some of the wives, telling them how much better their husbands would look with a fresh patch glued on top.

Wednesday October 15

Sure enough, Dan Prosser brought up the wig business at Council tonight! Accused Clipper of un-ethical business practice. Dan hasn't had a strand of hair for years. Since he hasn't much else going for him, I guess being the baldest man in town is sort of his pride and distinction.

You'd think Hetty, his wife, would know that. But then maybe she's just being smart; figuring that getting Old Baldy fuzzed over would clear the way for her to get a little fresh hair herself.

It made for an interesting meeting. I had to keep banging my gavel. I sure wish Clipper had been out fishing when that salesman came by!

Thursday October 16

Just at the close of last night's Council meeting, I slipped in a comment about the fact that next year we might have a new Mayor, if the people chose. Said I thought it would be only fair to them if we took a fresh look at our town's by-laws and constitution. Suggested we appoint a committee to do it.

This morning, I called Sim Jack, Jim Dupuis and Bill Huggins and invited them over to the house for this evening.

After a few drinks, we all agreed there are three things about elections that should be altered in our by-laws:
(1) The by-laws should be changeable by unanimous vote of Council.
(2) It should be possible for Council to demand an election at any time on a vote of confidence (in the Mayor).
(3) The Mayor's term of office should be set by Council.
It took almost the last of my scotch (and a lot of rye for Sim Jack), but we ended up agreeing heartily.

Friday October 17

It took four men and the town snow plow but we finally got those rocks in shape on each side of the town entrance. You still get the feeling you're driving into the mouth of the Lost Mine but once the girls get some evergreens planted it may look better.

I had forgotten that they would need earth as well as rocks. Solved that by moving the top of our ski slope out there. When we built the slope four years ago it seemed like a great idea. Unfortunately, it was only later we discovered that no one in town skis. Now, with its top shaved off, we have a nice toboggan run for the kids—and a rock garden too.

Meanwhile, everything at the sewage farm is in good shape and we're ready to hook up the system.

Saturday October 18

Big excitement today! Somehow, when Dusty was feeding the animals at the zoo, the lock on the lion's cage didn't catch. After Dusty had left, the lion pushed the door open and ambled off. First thing I knew about it was a frantic call from a voter out on the Back Road. He had been sitting in his outhouse with the door open, getting some sun, when suddenly the lion poked his head in. (I gather said voter was glad to be in place for the reaction that ensued.)

Next came a couple of other calls from hysterical folk. Then Jim Dupuis rang up to say they'd had a call at the Fire Department and asked what they should do. I couldn't find Dusty but told Jim to stop by and pick me up. We went tearing out to the Back Road and began to follow the trail. It was clearly marked by hysterical women. In the end, it led to Auntie Maude's place, and there the excitement ended. Auntie Maude had taken the poor beast in and shut it up with her dog and pony. She was real reluctant to give it back.

Sunday October 19

We let Auntie Maude keep the lion overnight—largely because we couldn't find Dusty and none of the rest of us were too inclined to get involved.

Dusty finally appeared about noon today, looking a little ragged from having slept off a bottle in his woodshed. Went out with him to Auntie Maude's to see what could be done. When the old girl saw me and knew we meant business, she gave in. "Mirabelle!" she called. "Give them back their damn lion!"

A girl I'd never seen before came out of the house and went right into Maude's pen. The dog and pony seemed very glad to see her. She went right up to the lion, took him by the mane and led him out. "Where do you want him?" she asked. "Back in his cage," I replied, adding "Please" kind of belatedly. She led the lion up the road (with us following at a respectful distance) and took him right into his cage without any trouble. She grinned at us both as she came out. "I sure wish you'd lend him to me sometime," she said. "It'd be a real money maker!"

Monday October 20

One of the unfortunate results of the lion incident was that Auntie Maude came in for a lot of public attention. Normally, you seldom hear her name mentioned. She runs a nice quiet house and minds her own business—and people like it that way. But she came out of the lion matter looking like a heroine.

If there's one thing a good, clean-living housewife can't stand, it's any sign of approval for any other woman. So I've had calls today from several good, clean-living housewives asking what I'm going to do about Auntie Maude? Well, maybe I will lend her the lion—and invite their husbands to the party.

Tuesday October 21

Should record for future reference that, in addition to yesterday's calls from housewives, had one this morning from Letty Hinch. Now there's a different kettle of fish!

Letty's approach was that Auntie Maude should be closed down because she isn't paying business taxes. It was a fresh idea. "Maybe we should charge her an equipment rental tax!" I said, but Letty either didn't get it or didn't want to.

Wednesday October 22

The Special Committee On Constitutional Reform (as I called it for the benefit of *The Portent*) brought in its report. Not unnaturally, Casey thought it was great. It was approved unanimously and my three changes are now law—and will be forever after, unless I want to alter them.

Now comes the hard part.

Thursday October 23

Went to see Casey today. Guess he knew by the way I closed his door it was a serious matter. Told him right out that I had heard he wanted to be Mayor. Added that I thought he'd make a good one.

Offered to help him get elected. But added I certainly didn't envy him his success. Said it wasn't just the cost of campaigning but the other costs, having to entertain and all. Then there was the time problem. Being the town banker and easily accessible, there would be a constant stream of people coming in about one thing and another.

This seemed to disturb him a little so I let it churn for a while before throwing in the salt: naturally, it wouldn't be ethical for the Mayor also to be handling loans to the town, issuing its bonds, etc. We would have to move all that to a bank in another town.

The thought of giving up money was, as I suspected, more than Casey could stand. He ended up pleading with me to run again. I said I'd consider it.

Friday October 24

Dusty called this morning and asked, "Have you got the car today?" I said I had. "Well," he says, "I think you and I should go for a little drive." Since I know Dusty uses other people's phones as he goes around inspecting, I didn't press him for details.

A little while later, he and I pulled up on the road that goes by the sewage plant. "What's this all about?" I demanded.

"Open your window and you'll find out." Got his message before the window was open more than an inch. And this is only the fourth day of operation!

"What are we going to do?" I cried. "Well," says Dusty, "first, I'd shut the window."

Saturday October 25

Had Casey over for a nice quiet drink this afternoon. We watched the football game for awhile and then sort of slid into the election business again. He asked me if I had decided yet whether to run again.

"No," I said, "I haven't. In fact, I think the only way I'd take it on would be with your help."

"What do you mean?" he says, sipping my scotch.

"Well," I says, creeping up on the idea gently, "I've always hated elections. And they're not too good for the town: expensive, unsettling. I think I've proven I can be a good Mayor. But this business of having to keep applying for the job I've already got seems pretty silly to me. I wish you could think of a way around it. There must be an answer, like in the Senate or something. . . ."

Casey examined the issue carefully. "As long as you're Mayor, my bank gets the town's business?" I nodded. "Well, then," says he very quietly, "why don't we just make you Mayor For Life?"

To show how moved I was by his idea I stood up and shook his hand. It's men like Casey who have made our town what it is today.

Sunday October 26

Al Pines grabbed me on the way out of church today. "Mr. Mayor," he says like a TV reporter, "we've had a report that there's a problem out at the sewage plant. Do you have any comment?"

"Well," says I—having watched a little TV myself, "let me say this about that. Having a sewer system in Upper Upsalquitch is a big step forward. And progress almost always brings with it some problems. If indeed there is one at the sewage plant, all I can say is that as soon as it is officially brought to our attention, we will take whatever steps are necessary to correct it."

Monday October 27

Jim Dupuis is a pretty sensible fellow. I'm so worried about that smell at the sewage plant (I drove out after dark last night and it is definitely getting worse), I feel I have to talk to somebody. I don't know whether being an undertaker makes Jim anything of an expert, but I figure at least here's one guy that can take it.

Called him this afternoon and told him that Al Pines had heard there was a problem. Asked him if, as Councillor and the Fire Chief, he would go out there with me to see what was going on.

Jim said sure for tomorrow morning, but he couldn't make it this afternoon. "I've just gotten a loved one in," he says, "and I've got to get to work. Business is getting a little stiff right now."

Tuesday October 28

A nice, clear, sunny fall day. The sort that makes a walk in the open air a joy. Except when you're inspecting a sewage plant. Jim and I got there in mid morning but didn't stay long. Hadn't walked more than twenty feet from the car when Jim said, "Come on, let's go!" We climbed back in and I pushed the car up to forty to clear out the smell.

"Well? What do you think it is?" I asked.

"Think? I know!" said Jim. "Didn't you ever wonder why our graveyards are so far from town? This whole area is sitting on rock, that's why. And we have to go miles to find earth deep enough for a burial. Whoever picked that spot for a sewage farm must have been crazy! What you've got there is a shallow rock tub. And the more people flush, the worse it's going to get. Give it a year and they'll be able to smell us in Boston!"

Wednesday October 29

Since the word (like the smell) is getting around, I knew that the topic would come up at tonight's Council meeting. Believing, like the mother skunk, that the best defence is offence, I beat them all to the punch by telling them that the matter had been drawn to my attention and that Jim Dupuis and I had gone there and could confirm that a problem existed.

"It sure as hell does!" said Jim. "And it's not going to get any better." My faithful band all looked at their fearless leader for guidance.

"Jim," I said. "I've been doing a great deal of thinking about this. You're right. Unless something is done we're all going to be victims of an ill wind. However, before we spend a lot of the taxpayers' money, I think we should wait a couple of weeks to see what develops."

"I can tell you what's going to develop," muttered Jim. But before he could get explicit I changed the subject.

Thursday October 30

Jim Dupuis called this morning. "What are you up to?" he demanded. "About what?" I hedged. "About that damn sewer farm, that's what! You know waiting for two weeks isn't going to improve things. You're in trouble, my friend! If an election was coming up right now you'd lose in a landslide of shit."

I sighed. "Jim, you're sure short on faith in your friends! Tell you what, you and I'll go out to that farm again in two weeks time and if the odour hasn't gone away, I'll resign and you can be Mayor."

"To hell with that for a deal," says Jim. "Being an undertaker is bad enough."

Hallowe'en

Friday October 31

Felt kind of awkward tonight. Annie threw a Hallowe'en party and invited me. It's the first time I've been in Casey's house since we held that secret meeting two years ago when Clare Latrouche announced she was going to run for Council.

Annie not only coaxed me into going, she got me to dress up. She wanted to be Cinderella and nothing would do but that I should be Prince Charming. I finally said, "All right. So long as princes can wear plus-fours." Annie went right to the encyclopedia and showed me a picture of a prince. Damned if he wasn't wearing them!

Big party. Didn't know Annie had so many friends. Tried to be a good sport. Went around urging the ladies to try on one of Annie's plastic slippers. Because of my girth, found it exhausting to keep going down to defeat.

Affairs of this kind are not my happiest times. Have always felt a little out of place. I try to be jolly, tell a few stories, try a few puns. But usually my stories fall flat and my puns go unnoticed. Like tonight when I tried to tell them how the story of Cinderella really ended: the prince found her and married her and soon after became a pauper. Thud.

Saturday November 1

All Saints preserve us! I have been asked to speak next week to the public school children. "A Message From The Mayor." What do you say to the kids that trampled your rose bushes all summer?

If I'm frank, they'll snivel all the way home and lose me votes. If I'm trite, they'll yawn. If I tell them I love them, I'll never see a rose bush in bloom again.

Sunday November 2

Hetty Prosser stopped me as I was leaving church today and asked what I was going to do about wintering the animals at the zoo. Why is it always me? Sometimes, I feel like answering the "What am I going to do?" with "Not a God damn thing!"

However, she has a point. I guess where elephants and lions come from this would be regarded as a pretty cold day. Hell, this is a cold day no matter where you come from! The TV says it's going to warm up tonight but that won't last. "O.K., Mr. Mayor, where do elephants go in the winter time?" Ah me! I'll have to sleep on that one!

Monday November 3

Finally, a bit of good weather! Actually quite mild for this time of year when we usually get a blast or two of early snow.

Called Dusty and got him to come over for a consultation. After I applied a little persuasion (because he was slow to see the merit and supreme logic), he went away to get the materials he needed—and probably to have a bit of sleep before tackling the only possible solution to the sewage farm odour problem.

I don't envy him having to work in the dark. But this is not a matter that would benefit from public attention.

Tuesday November 4

Along about noon I finally heard from Dusty. He had just gotten out of bed and still sounded pretty groggy. However, he reported that Operation De-smell was completed—and without any known observers.

"Good work!" I exclaimed. "Now why don't you go down to Sim Jack's, have a good meal and charge it to me?"

Dusty made a choking noise. "What's the matter?" I asked. "Food!" he exclaimed. "I won't be able to eat again for a year! I think I'll have to take a bath in turpentine or something to get that smell off my skin!"

Wednesday November 5

Gambled on being seen and took a run out to the sewage farm this afternoon. It's still pretty early to tell, but I think Dusty has licked the problem.

Went to Council with a light heart. Was able to assure them that the sewage situation was well on the way to being cured. When Jim Dupuis asked how, said that I had believed all along that it was only a question of time.

If they ever discover how the problem really got solved, I may get into trouble. But it's better to gamble on *that* than live with the sure thing that the growing smell could ruin my career.

Getting Dusty to hook up the pipe to the river again was the only possible solution. But from now on I think I'd better boil my drinking water.

Thursday November 6

I sure feel slow-witted sometimes! Here I've been worrying since Sunday about where to put the zoo for winter—and all along the right answer was staring at me: Dusty Miller's place. He's got a big shed out back of his house that will take all the cages nicely. Be real handy for him when it comes to caring for them.

May be a bit noisy for his neighbours at times with the elephant trumpeting, the lion roaring and those striped donkeys braying. But I'm sure they'll get used to it.

Friday November 7

Well, I survived. I think. Today was Civics Day at the school. I put on my robe of office (an old bathrobe Annie dyed black) and my chain (the dining-room chandelier looks better close to the ceiling) and off I went to deliver the promised speech.

Decided to give it to them straight. The truth and nothing but the truth. "The children of today are the adults of tomorrow." That shook them.

However, must admit there was one thing that made my performance a little less than perfect. As I talked it seemed they were being more attentive than usual. Felt flattered. It was only after I was off stage that I discovered that my robe had been hanging open and that in my rush to get there I had forgotten to do up my fly. (Hope I didn't damage any young ids.)

Saturday November 8

Was asked to open the Women's Guild Charity Bazaar this morning. *I* tried to be charitable, and *it* certainly was bizarre.

Hard put to understand why Letty Hinch rushed to buy the first ticket in the draw for a lace blouse. I've heard of the merits of "see-through" blouses. But on Letty you'd be better off not.

Sunday November 9

Casey caught me on the way out of church and asked if he could see me. Came over about three.

I had told him we had to force a vote of confidence and pull a fast election. Now, he wanted to tell me he had been thinking about it and had decided I was wrong. "We don't need it," he says. "Look, Mr. Mayor, we've known each other a long time. I think you respect me; maybe you even trust me a little, though there's lots don't. Will you trust me in this? I think I can swing it."

"What do I have to do?" I asked.

"Nothing. That's important. Not a damn thing. No matter what you hear, don't hear it. Just play dumb and let it happen to you. Okay?"

Well, that isn't exactly my nature, I wanted to say. But I sensed he had put a lot of thought into the matter. And I can always jump in if he starts to pull a fast one.

Monday November 10

The animals are all snugly established in Dusty's big shed. Mrs. Miller is a real mouse and, outside of a sigh that seemed to start at her toes, gave no sign of objection when I dropped over to see them about it.

Actually, it was Dusty that gave me a little trouble but I pointed out that he was the only man in town who really knew the animals well enough to be trusted with them. He conceded I was right. Then I asked him where else we could put them that would be handy for him when the snow got four feet deep. His shed began to look good.

Finally, I told him that if he wanted to charge admission and keep the proceeds it would be all right with me. I saw Mrs. Miller brighten a shade. I think the first thing they will want to buy with the money is a big fan.

Remembrance Day

Tuesday November 11

Today, all across Canada it's Remembrance Day. Troops parade, a moment of silence is observed, and we remember those who gave their lives for their country.

We don't have any troops in Upper Upsalquitch. But there are enough veterans to make a showing and we throw in the Boy Scouts and Girl Guides for good measure.

There's no real cenotaph but years ago someone put up a cement cross on the front lawn of what is now the United Church and we use that.

As the senior official, I have to lay the first wreath. I must say, those plastic flowers we're bringing in from Saint John looked just fine. (And they're so light they make the wreathes very easy to handle.)

Wednesday November 12

Haven't heard a word more from Casey about the election plan. I had the distinct feeling he was avoiding me at Council tonight.

When I got back, I asked Annie to keep her ears open around home. If anyone said anything about elections I wanted to know what it was right away.

"Is anything wrong?" she asked, concerned.

"No," I said, "but there could be." In this business you're always living on the edge of danger.

Thursday November 13

I've done it again. Another year has rolled around and I've left it too late to get my Christmas cards free. If I would just face up to it in, say, October I could write to all the card houses the way I used to and get enough samples to see me through.

Of course, there's one good thing about it; I don't have to put up with all those dunning letters later asking how many I sold.

But here I am, cardless. And every year the mailing list gets longer and longer. The more people owe money for back taxes, the more cards I get. And since they're voters as well as debtors, the more I have to send out. Looking at it that way, it's a town problem. So I'd better have a word with our genial Treasurer soon.

Friday November 14

Insurance is the price of insecurity. Luckily, there are a lot of insecure people in Upper Upsalquitch. If only they were better off! The size of the average life policy here is so low that it's really a death policy; just big enough to get them buried. (In all honesty, when I look at some of the heirs-to-be, I can understand the reluctance to leave them anything.)

Until recently, the only person I had to give a thought to in terms of my own leftovers was Cousin Ralph. The rest of the family is long gone. And Ralph seems to be doing all right on his own. But now I find myself thinking about Annie.

For some reason, I'd like to do something for her. Not that she will ever need money. As Casey's only heir she'll probably be president of the bank someday.

In view of *that* and since she is so good about typing all of my policies, I think I'll take out a policy for her. She deserves it.

Saturday November 15

Snow flurries this morning but the sun came out by noon and the rest of the day was fine. Picked up Annie and took her out for a drive. Stopped in the country to collect some premium payments.

Told her I was planning to take out a policy in her name. "You mean a genuine policy—with the company?"

"That's right. The real thing!"

"But won't that be very expensive?"

"I don't know," I admitted frankly.

After a bit she said, "Why are you doing this?"

"Why? Because I want to. Because we've become very close and I want to provide for you. You're like a daughter to me!"

She turned and looked at me. "I'm glad you never married!"

Sunday November 16

Casey Irving took up the collection in church this morning. When he came to my row he wouldn't look at me, even though I did put something in the plate.

There's more going on here than is willing to meet the eye.

Monday November 17

Joe Azar came into Sim Jack's this morning. Got him off in a corner and talked over the Christmas card problem. Asked me right off how much it would take out of the town funds to buy the cards and mail them. Borrowed Sim's phone and called Al Pines. Inquired what Al charges for a page. Turned out to be half the total I had given Joe.

"Now," says Joe, "Here's what you do: write a nice Christmas message, saying that this year instead of spending money on cards you are going to give it to charity."

"You mean like UNICEF or CARE?"

"Well," says Joe, "I wouldn't be that specific. I mean charity begins at home. Right?"

As a Treasurer, Joe is coming along nicely. You've got to hand it to him on this one. So I did: another cup of coffee.

Tuesday November 18

Annie got her policy all typed today and I signed it. Made out the medical form myself. Sent the whole thing off with a note asking them to deduct the premiums from my commissions. (That way, I won't have to pay tax on the money.)

Wrote it up as a straight life policy but made sure it was convertible. If Annie ever left me, I'd sure hate to lose the money I'm putting in. This way, I can elect to take it out in pension.

Wednesday November 19

Proposed to Council an idea which has been forming in my mind for some time. Upper Upsalquitch has never had a motto.

At first, I tried to think up one on my own but decided we could get a lot of good mileage out of calling for suggestions from the taxpayers. This led to the concept of having a contest.

For some reason, Council took the idea rather lightly at first. Bill Huggins suggested that the prizes be free trips away from Upper Upsalquitch. Sim Jack said maybe our motto should be "The Best Is Yet To Come"—but I told him he should save that for his menus. The meeting finally fell apart—but we *are* going to have the contest.

Thursday November 20

Al Pines came in to see me today about the motto contest. He's all enthused. After the meeting last night, Sim Jack volunteered to give a free dinner-for-two as a prize and Ned Dervish agreed to throw in two free tickets to the movies. Some lucky winner is going to have a hot time on the old town one night.

Al thought it would be good to start the contest off by having leading citizens give examples, so he got on my phone and called around. Jim Dupuis, (the undertaker side of him taking over) suggested "We Live Gravely." Bill Huggins took time off from mixing pills to suggest "The Elixir City"—which sounds kind of fancy. Casey Irving suggested "Invest In Tomorrow." Turning to local industry, Al called Auntie Maude who (he assured me) suggested *"Per Ardour Ad Astra."* The Reverend Angus leaned on his Golden Rule: "Do Unto More People . . ." and so on. Hope the common folks have more of the bard in them.

Friday November 21

Be darned if I don't begin to see what Casey is up to on the election business. *The Portent* had a big article in it on how wasteful it is to keep having elections. Then it went on to say it was bad how good men often lose their jobs in elections. Then, by golly, it got right down to brass tacks and mentioned me! "What a shame it would be if this dedicated citizen were to cease to be our Mayor!" It mentioned how I worked full time at it without pay. And then sort of clinched things by suggesting that if we got a new Mayor we'd probably have to pay him—and that would mean higher taxes.

A great opening move. Having promised to play dumb, I can't say anything but I'm dying to know what some people think.

Saturday November 22

Al called about the motto contest. I tried to get him to say something about the article on mayors but he was very evasive. Maybe it's too soon for reaction.

Meantime, plowing along the slogan route, Father Ignatius has suggested "Up Upper Upsalquitch"—which is kind of bright, although it does have overtones he may have missed.

Joe Azar thinks it would be good to choose *Caveat Emptor*. I don't think he knows what that means any more than I do so I countered with *Cave Filia Canum*, which I believe is the motto of some big advertising agency.

Sunday November 23

Casey's back to his old tricks. Wouldn't look at me when he passed the plate at church again this morning.

I always say if there's one place where people should at least try to be honest with each other it's in church. After all, it's only for one hour a week. And you have the rest of the week to be yourself.

Maybe that article in *The Portent* was just a trick. Or (even worse), maybe he's got the idea that he will run for Mayor after all—and then use the Mayor-For-Life idea for himself.

Monday November 24

After an unsettled night dreaming about Casey, awoke wondering why there isn't such a thing as unemployment insurance for Mayors. For that matter, maybe what we need is group job insurance for Councillors, too, but I'll worry about them later. Right now, *I'm* all the problem I can handle.

Think I'll write to Perpetual Life and see if there's any policy that fits my need. The only thing is how do I collect—and *how much* do I collect—if I get thrown out of a job that doesn't pay anything?

Tuesday November 25

Got the furnace going today. Always postpone it as long as possible not only because coal is so expensive now but it's a messy job.

However, Annie said she didn't relish having to make dinner with her overcoat on so I gave in. People are getting soft. When I was a boy we got through the winter with just the help of the kitchen stove and a big round monster in the front hall that was called a "Franklin" (presumably because old Benjamin was pot-bellied too). The pipes from both of these wandered around a bit before they made it to the chimney and spread heat as they went.

Today, I have to go to the basement, jerk a handle back and forth to clear out ashes, throw in some paper and kindling, then shovel heaps of dusty coal and pray. If the fire catches, we get heat coming up through the big register in the front hall. If it doesn't, I have to go down into the depths and start all over again.

New Brunswick coal leaves something to be desired: *an oil burner.*

Wednesday November 26

At Council meeting Casey asked (and got) permission to read into the Minutes the article from *The Portent* on elections "as a tribute to our Mayor."

Everyone applauded, which was nice. But I can't see why he did it. However, since he winked at me during the applause I'm sure he had his reasons. Felt a little better about him than I did Sunday.

Thursday November 27

Despite being a little reassured by Casey's speech, I got off that letter to the insurance company today asking if they had a policy to cover me if I lose. Suggested that there might be something under "Casualty" that applied.

I sure hope the company answers soon. Time is running out.

Friday November 28

The Portent this week carries a front page story on the motto contest. I guess Al wrote the rules as he went. He has given the readers a two-week deadline. Couldn't help noticing that all entries are to be addressed to *The Portent* and that he never got around to mentioning it was my idea.

When he phoned this afternoon to see what I thought of the story, I complimented him profusely, then mentioned that it would be nice if, in the next issue, he happened to mention that I thought it all up.

"Hell, Mayor!" he cried. "You don't want that! There could be a real hassle over this if people don't like the motto chosen. With the election coming up, I thought you'd want to stay out of this!" Had to admit he had a point—even if I suspect he thought it up as he was talking to me.

Saturday November 29

Went over to Dusty's place to check on the zoo. Mrs. Miller seemed a little cool, I thought, though it was hard to tell since she wouldn't speak to me.

Dusty was out loading his wheelbarrow. He's getting quite a pile behind the shed and I can see that Mrs. Miller, who goes out there to hang up her laundry, may feel that a better solution could have been found. However, when she sees what a wonderful garden they're going to have next year she may feel better.

That stuff is especially great for rhubarb. I remember that Grandma's rhubarb patch was always located wherever the outhouse had been the year before.

Sunday November 30

On the way into church today, picked up a magazine in the anthrax, published by the Head Office boys and full of great Christian injunctions like leaving some of your money to them.

Took the paper to my pew and read while waiting for the Reverend Angus to get up his nerve to come out and face us. Spotted an interesting ad for collection plates. Our plates are old brass things—and very noisy. The ad offers ones with velvet-covered bottoms.

This being Saint Andrew's Day, beloved of Scots, it did not seem unreasonable to sit there doing some canny thinking. Figured that if I were to donate a set of those plates to our church, I would have my money back in just under three years by what I'd save through being able to drop in smaller coins. Have always resented having my Christian charity measured in decibels.

Monday December 1

Clare Latrouche telephoned this evening just as Annie and I were cleaning vegetables for dinner. Very untimely. Always make a point of helping Annie with the vegetables. If I don't, she takes the skins right off them—and that's where all the vitamins are. Have tried to explain to her that at my age I really need all the vitamins I can get.

Anyway, I hope I wasn't short with Clare. All she wanted to know was whether I would mind if at the next Council meeting she proposed a poll tax. Told her it was all right by me, but I couldn't support her. "Why not?" she demanded, sounding a mite hurt.

I didn't want to tell her there was no way I was going to get tarred with a new tax just before election. All I could think to say was, "I don't believe in racial discrimination."

Tuesday December 2

Just when you think you have everything under control, all hell breaks loose.

Was sitting in my office today minding my own business when Dusty came bursting in with bad news. (Good news doesn't have as much kinetic energy as bad news.) Somebody from somewhere else must have used the Tourist Attraction, and as a result such local citizens as are brave enough to use it in this weather have contracted a "social" disease. Well, we've taken everything else the Americans have to offer, I suppose this sort of completes the package!

I told Dusty how to clean up the Attraction. But I'm at a bit of a loss on how to clean up the citizens. I guess they'll just have to scratch for themselves.

Wednesday December 3

Got ahold of Al Pines first thing this morning and explained the health problem. We don't know who all has used the can but the way those bugs spread we could soon have the whole town infected.

Suggested that rather than make a fuss and get everybody upset, he should run a sort of medical column giving the cure—and let it go at that. Told Al, however, that he should check with the hospital to see if they couldn't suggest something professional-sounding.

Thursday December 4

For the first time in many a winter we had to cancel a Council meeting last night. A bad storm came swooping down on us from Squaw Cap Mountain just before supper time last night. Lashing winds and wet snow that turned to ice. Both cars parked outside are frozen in place.

Along about seven, the power went out. Since there was nothing to be gained (and perhaps a great deal to be lost) from meeting in the dark, I called the boys and told them to stay home. Being as nervous as I am about the election, that was the only logical course of action. The power came back on this morning—but it looks as though I am going to be kept in the dark for another whole week!

Friday December 5

Al Pines ran another feature on the motto contest this week. He's having a ball. The mottoes suggested by leading citizens will make any entry look good. I'm just glad he didn't quote me.

Got a great kick out of his prize list. Beside the offer of dinner-for-two he ran a picture of what must have been a royal banquet—tall silver candlesticks and all. And beside the theatre ticket offer, he had found and run a picture of Grauman's Chinese Theatre in Hollywood.

I don't know how Ned Dervish will take the kidding about his theatre but I know Sim Jack is taking the meal seriously. When I went in for coffee this morning I found him reading "100 New Ways to Serve Rice."

Saturday December 6

That storm last Wednesday brought down a couple of fine trees. It's a real shame. After Dusty got through cutting them up and hauling them off the streets I went around to the back of my shed to look at them. Close to two cord of fine firewood, but at what a price!

We Upper Upsalquitchers have always been proud of our tree-lined streets. In the Spring I think I'll organize a committee to plant new trees.

Sunday December 7

Had a very unusual experience today: went to the R.C. Church. Father Ignatius thought it would be nice in this pre-Christmas season if the Mayor were to pay a visit. Not only that, he got me up in the pulpit to read a lesson! That's more than the Reverend Angus has done in a long while!

Thought I would feel pretty uncomfortable but when I looked down at the congregation I was so fascinated I forgot to be nervous. I'd never realized before how many people I know are R.C.'s. My father had brought me up to believe that you could always tell a Catholic just by looking at him.

Monday December 8

Bill Ellis was waiting for me when I got to Sim Jack's this morning. I figured it must be something serious to take him away from his school on a Monday morning, so I led him back to one of the rear booths.

He got into it right away. Wanted my advice on what to do with his pregnant students. Seems our pleasant, warm summer's effect is starting to show in earnest and some of the girls aren't going to make it even to Easter. "It gets worse every year," he muttered. "Used to be one or two girls might get in trouble. They'd decide to leave school quietly and never be seen again. But now you'd think promiscuity was a hobby! Instead of recess, we have to give time off for morning sickness!"

"Well," I said, "seems to me, Bill, you can't fight human nature. But, you might try de-grading it."

"Oh?" he said, looking a little shocked.

"That's what it needs," I assured him. "De-grade your sex education course from high school to elementary. That way you get to play teacher while they're still playing doctor."

172

Tuesday December 9

It is one of those nights when dim December threatens to breathe its killing chills upon the head or heart. Sitting close to the fire, wrapped in my bathrobe, my Romeos and knees are a bit warmer than the rest of me. My diary is on my lap and my head is bent over it as I try to write by the light of the flames.

I could go downstairs and put more coal in the furnace. I could turn on the lights. I could even put down this ledger of my days and assume the national slouch in front of the television set.

But after dinner I made a mistake. I read a little poetry by Stevenson, a bit by Poe. Now, my mind is moving too fast for television. I'm not in the mood to move through time at Big Brother's pace.

Thoughts of December, of my own December, lead not unnaturally to the days after. I wonder about those I will spend in the cemetery. Should I arrange now for a stone? No, I think not. It is better simply to leave instructions for the wording on it and hope that someone else will pay for it.

What should it say? The name, the dates, then something short and pertinent. Perhaps . . .

> *He strove for good*
> *And now he's gone for it.*

. . . or . . .

> *Think, stranger, as you pause to read*
> *Of who lies here. In word and deed*
> *He sought to be the perfect Mayor*
> *And, in truth, was always fair.*

Don't seem to be able to hit the rite note. My problem is that even on a dark night like this I am enjoying life so much that I can't take the prospect of death very seriously.

Perhaps I'll just leave a request that they inscribe my name and then, down low where the dogs can read it, add "Please!"

Wednesday December 10

At Council meeting tonight got a lot of compliments on my Christmas message in *The Portent*.

A pretty good meeting, overall. Only dark note was another one of those letters from Letty Hinch suggesting that we add a couple of books to the library. It's amazing how easy it is for people to think up ways for us to spend money!

I figure we have to have a library, in case Andrew Carnegie decides to check. But there's no point in embarrassing Bill Huggins by asking him to give us more shelf space.

Thursday December 11

The column on curing "the disease" must be having its effect. Checked with Bill Huggins and he tells me he had to order in extra ingredients. Dusty tells me someone clipped out the column and tacked it up on the door of the Attraction. Bill Ellis says some kid put it up on the school bulletin board.

On the theory that maybe cleanliness is after all next to godliness, I was going to have reprints made and put in the church pews but Annie talked me out of that. She said the waves of coughing that sweep over the congregation are bad enough.

Friday December 12

The Portent this week carried the final entries in the motto contest. None of them have seemed very exciting to me. But Al has done a smart thing: called for the readers to be judges and mail in their votes. This will stretch the matter out until after the election, which is fine by me! Perhaps when that's over I'll be able to come up with something suitable myself. We'll worry *then* about how to win a contest you never entered.

Saturday December 13

Met Hetty Prosser at market this morning. Covered the weather pretty thoroughly. At this time of year there isn't much you can say for it but there sure is a lot you can say about it.

Then, out of the blue (!), she asked, "You *are* going to go on being Mayor, aren't you?"

"Well, I suppose so," I replied, "assuming the people want me."

"Oh yes," she said. "There's that, isn't there?" Then she bustled away without another word, leaving me standing there between the frozen fish and the preserves.

Have never been this close to an election date before without knowing the outcome pretty well. Trouble is, this time I don't even know the in-go. It's unsettling.

Sunday December 14

Took a bit of teasing when I got to church today. The word had gotten around I had visited the R.C.'s last Sunday. In addition, Al Pines had taken a picture of me and Father Ignatius and run it in *The Portent*. Since the good Father had loaned me a surplus surplice which came way below my knees, you got the feeling from the picture that I didn't have on any pants at all. With my rather pronounced proboscis, plus the fact that I had neglected to remove my cap at that point, I looked like a giant female woodpecker.

Annie says I'm too hard on myself; anyone looking at the picture would know it was me. "After all," she said reassuringly, "who else could it be?"

Monday December 15

Sure miss not being able to go for a drive in the country! The car has snow tires, but even so there is always a good chance of getting stuck and I have no desire to spend the last minutes of my life freezing to death in a hearse!

Tuesday December 16

Saw an article in a magazine today that said the insurance business is going to suffer in the years ahead because the government is taking over. So far, outside of medicare, we haven't seen any sign of it down here. But perhaps I ought to be getting ready.

If I continue as Mayor I think I'll try to work up a townwide plan where people buy insurance the way they pay taxes. We might even be able to make insurance compulsory! The very thought of that makes my fingers tingle! I'd be so rich I could build a house on a *hil'* on Knob Hill! Maybe I'd hire Casey Irving as my butler!

Wednesday December 17

Was greatly relieved last Wednesday because Clare Latrouche didn't bring up the poll tax issue. But tonight she did—a whole week closer to the election! It really stumped me. Didn't want any discussion of new taxes with Al Pines sitting there making notes.

Luckily, Jim Dupuis saw my problem. Said that instead of a poll tax perhaps what we needed was a "clothespole" tax to discourage women from hanging out washing. It was impairing the attractiveness of our town. In addition, the distraction of women's undies flapping in the breeze constituted a traffic hazard.

Sim Jack, eager for laundry business, supported him strongly. Bill Huggins, who sells soap, fought back. Clare said something rude in French. Joe Azar, whose wife makes *him* do the laundry, gave what was probably a good translation in opposing her.

Had to bang my gavel for order. Finally, Jim said he'd withdraw his proposal if she'd withdraw hers and the meeting ended as a washout.

Thursday December 18

Had an idea while shaving this morning. Next year, this town is going to have a Santa Claus! Don't know how I'm going to arrange it, but whether I'm still Mayor or not I'm going to see to it that our kids are exposed to a real live man in red with a white beard. Doubt if we can swing a parade the way they do in the big cities but it shouldn't be hard to find someone who'll stuff a pillow in his pants for an hour or so and walk up and down crying "Ho! Ho! Ho!"

Suspect that most children don't actually believe in Santa anymore. But they do believe in the spirit of Christmas he represents. Santa appeals to the symbol-minded.

Friday December 19

There are enough supporters around of the R.C. tradition for Sim Jack still to feature fish on his Friday menus. Since my coffee visit sort of ran over into the lunch hour today, I accepted Sim's kind offer to stay.

However, I boggled at the prospect of fish, being a bit chary now of anything that floats in our river. Finally, I asked Sim what kind of fish he was serving. "Sole," he replied proudly, "all sole. Sorry. Maybe more tomorrow. You want eggs?"

Saturday December 20

How the year rolls around! Once again, it's ice fishing time and I'm having to dust off all the old excuses. This winter, however, I'm going to be more adamant than ever before. As I noted yesterday, the more I hear and see about pollution, the less inclined I am to trust anything from around this area.

If I ever come up with a better solution to our problems, my attitude may change. But not for at least one whole generation of fish.

Sunday December 21

How ironic that as we are about to experience the shortest day of the year, the Reverend Angus should give us his longest sermon! However, you have to forgive him a little. It's the Sunday before Christmas. His last chance to get the voice of the church heard above the noise of the cash registers.

As if to remind him of his competition, there was a beautiful big tree set up by the pulpit, decorated quite prettily by the Ladies' Aid. Was disturbed by one red light that kept blinking on and off. Reminded me of Auntie Maude and caused some irreverent thoughts.

The sermon was on the background for the Nativity scene. Extensive quotations from a book called "The Otherwise Man." All about an otherwise wise man who didn't get there in time to crêche the party.

The Reverend read from Matthew about the trip to Jerusalem. Have always had trouble with Matthew's approach to the whole thing. You don't find old Doctor Luke saying it the same way. But Matthew, after listing the begats with a tax collector's thoroughness, gets pretty confused and spills the whole story about the conception. Doc Luke is my boy; a physician can't afford to be as mixed up as the publican.

Monday December 22

Decided today was the day to get my Christmas tree. When I was a boy we used to make a family expedition of it, going out to the woods and hunting for the best one we could find. It's not like that anymore. The woods are all fenced and every farmer has his trees counted. Besides, I'm a little old to go wandering around in the woods with an axe.

Called Dusty and gave him the assignment. Late this afternoon he showed up with a beauty. It is the first time that I have ever had a Christmas tree with the roots still on it. Dusty pointed out that it would stay fresher that way, especially if I kept it watered. And, anyway, the roots would be needed later to hold it up when he replaced it in the rock garden at the entrance to town. Very smart pre-election thinking on his part. It had never occurred to me to put it back.

Tuesday December 23

Yesterday was the start of Christmas holidays for the school-aged. All day, there has been laughter in the streets. Plodding through snow to and from Sim Jack's, I was passed by groups in scarves and sniffles who eyed my headgear sadly because it sits so firmly.

Like my plus-fours my cap is a great and cherished find. It's of some soft, grey cloth and pulls right down, has peaks at the front and back and large earflaps which tie beneath my chin.

Annie says I look like Sherlock Holmes in summer (when the flaps are tied up) and like a bassett hound when the flaps are down. But I don't care. I'm warm and comfortable and smug in my knowledge that I'm frustrating the snowball set.

Wednesday December 24

Being Christmas Eve, no Council meeting tonight. Had hoped Annie
would stay on after work or come back to visit. But I understand.
It's a night for families to be together, even the Irvings. The season
of giving must be awfully hard on Casey's nerves.

Went to bed early. Then realized I had forgotten to bring my diary
up to date. Sorry, old friend! But must make it short. It is a custom
left from childhood to be asleep on Christmas Eve by midnight.

Just about the only custom I have left.

> *My stockings are hung by the chimney with care.*
> *With knowledge they'll probably dry faster there.*

Christmas Day

Thursday December 25

Merry Christmas to me! Arose late and padded around the house
until noon. Then went down to Sim Jack's for my annual turkey
dinner. Have had better—but the price was right.

Annie came by for a while this afternoon. Brought me a pair of
socks she had knitted herself. They say of gifts that it's the thought
that counts. In this case, I suspect the thought is that since they are too
short to go with my plus-fours I'll have to put on trousers once in a
while just to get some wear out of them.

Gave her a lace shawl that belonged to my mother. It hadn't been
worn very often and is in pretty good shape. Lest Annie think me
parsimonious—a trait that her background has taught her to be quick
to recognize—I wrote a little note to go in the parcel:

> This shawl belonged to a wonderful woman, my mother. Of all
> the women I have met since her, you are the only fitting one to
> wear it.

I hope that didn't sound ꞏꞈꞈ sentimental. She read it a couple of
times, so I guess it made an impression.

Friday December 26

They call this Boxing Day because in England boxes are given to
errand boys, postmen and those who are entitled to gratuities. Not a
Canadian custom, thank goodness. Just an extra holiday to pad out
the Christmas season.

It is also Saint Stephen's Day. He was the first of the Christian
martyrs. The Bible says that one of his persecutors was a young
fellow named Saul, who later became the Apostle Paul. Paul, as I
understand it, is credited with founding the Catholic Church and
getting the Vatican in business. Just shows what a good Jewish boy
can do if he changes his name.

Saturday December 27

A listless day. A good Mayor knows when to stay out of sight. And
this long, family weekend is no time for me to be charging around
trying to stir up votes for the election. It is hard to keep quiet. The
ticking of the big clock in the kitchen can be heard all over the house.
Time is passing. The election is getting closer.

As if to try and hold time back, I took down the clock and gave the
case and face a thorough cleaning. It is something I've been meaning
to do for a long time, ever since I brought it here from the railway
station when they discontinued service. Seems just too few people
wanted to come here, and no one here could afford to leave.

Unfortunately, the time spent cleaning was time standing still.
There was a snow storm today and the power is off. I'll have to wait
for it to come on before I can find out from the radio or TV how much
time I've lost. It's like living in limbo.

Sunday December 28

The new collection plates I ordered for the church arrived this week and were used today. The Reverend Angus thanked me very nicely from the pulpit and people turned around and smiled with what I hope were looks of appreciation.

With some apprehension, when the plate on my aisle reached me I dropped in a large coin and a small. Both seemed to make about the same dull clunk, so my gamble has paid off and I can relax. Now, all I have to remember is to give the plate a little shake as I pass it so that no one can spot which dime is mine.

After the service, gathered up the old brass plates and took them home. Stood them on edge on the mantel over the fireplace where they look very nice indeed. They not only add warmth to the room but will also help remind me always to have the right change on Sundays.

Monday December 29

To my surprise, Casey telephoned this morning. Said that the Councillors would like to meet tomorrow night since Wednesday is New Year's Eve.

Seemed like a reasonable suggestion. Last time we met on New Year's Eve Dan Prosser brought his guitar. Things got a bit out of hand. Remembering that, I hastened to agree.

Then Casey got into a rigmarole about town funds. Not the sort of thing I like to discuss on the party line or with his heir apparent, Annie, sitting right beside me at her typewriter. He said Upper Upsalquitch needed a lot of major improvements and the way to pay for them was with a bond issue. Mentioned a rate of interest so high I thought he was quoting his age.

Finally, I said, "Look, Casey, you know that if the town does any borrowing it will be from you. But I can't commit myself until after we get the election issue settled."

He sort of laughed. "That's all I want to hear, Mr. Mayor!"

After he hung up I began to get that wonderful feeling that somehow I could make a deal. Began to look forward to Council meeting.

Tuesday December 30

Tonight, as soon as I had banged my gavel to call the meeting to order, Casey got to his feet and said he wanted to talk about elections.

"I have here," he said, producing a big roll of paper, "a petition signed by the majority of the voters. It asks that the town be spared the cost of an election and that our present Mayor be continued in office. I may say," he went on, glancing meaningfully at me, "that I had a conversation with our Mayor yesterday. He has indicated that subject to certain conditions he would be willing to accept the wishes of the people."

"What conditions?" Jim Dupuis asked.

I cleared my throat. "Well, principally, that you will all support me in a program to make this a better town. We won't go into details tonight, but I believe the time has come to invest against the future."

The Council voted unanimously to recognize the petition and be governed by it.

Afterward, got Casey in a corner. "That was quite a feat," I complimented him, "getting that petition signed!"

"Well," he said cautiously, "I wouldn't want to unroll it too far. I think I'll just put it in the bank safe until we need it again. So far as I am concerned, it applies from now on. Which means," he added pointedly, "that so long as there are bond issues annually you can regard yourself as Mayor-For-Life."

Wednesday December 31

Walking home last night, felt as happy as Auntie Maude when a bus pulls up.

This morning, however, saw the truth. I had what I wanted—but Casey had me. I would have to do something—and fast—to get him under control.

Before Annie left, invited her to come back and see in the New Year with me. By the time she returned, I had bathed and shaved and even put on a pair of trousers. No champagne so made do with rye.

After midnight turned off the TV, put my arm around her and said I had something to ask.

She looked kind of apprehensive. "What is it?"

Stammered a lot but finally got it out. Almost before I had finished she cried "YES!" and kissed me. Had to promise to burn my plus-fours, of course. But, all considered, that's a small concession.

What a great way to start the New Year!